A WOMAN'S PLACE

Relationship Breakdown and Your Rights
A Guide for Married Women

Revised by Julie Bull, Sue Spaull
and Lorraine Thompson

SHAC
189a Old Brompton Road
London SW5 0AR

SHAC

SHAC opened in 1969 as London's first independent housing aid centre. Its work covers the whole range of housing problems, including homelessness, security of tenure, disrepair and mortgage arrears. Over the past 20 years SHAC has given advice and help to over 120,000 households.

SHAC's publications and training courses draw on this direct advice-giving experience. SHAC produces a range of rights guides, publishes research into major housing issues and provides information and training for a wide range of voluntary and statutory organisations.

For further information about SHAC publications, contact the Publications Officer; for details of training courses, contact the training department.

A Woman's Place

ISBN   0 948857 26 9

© **SHAC, 1989**

Design, Typesetting and Artwork by LASSO Co-operative

Printing by RAP Limited

SHAC receives financial support from the Department of the Environment, the London Borough Grants Unit and many other public authorities and private corporate donors.

Acknowledgements

This book is a revised and updated version of the first edition. The authors thank its author Sue Witherspoon.

In preparing this book the authors gratefully acknowledge the help of the following people:
Angela Hadjipateras, Helen McKenna, John Gallagher, Sara Evans, Barbara Hurst, Kay Hart and Christine Jamieson.

Contents

Introduction

If you are married and your relationship breaks down, there will often be all sorts of practical as well as emotional problems for you to deal with. This book is intended to help you sort some of these practical problems and to understand what rights you have in relation to:

☐ money

☐ housing

☐ children

The guide is written for women and so it explains the law from this point of view – although in many cases legal rights will apply to both you and your ex-husband. The law is complicated and always changing, so we don't advise you to use the book as a substitute for proper advice but we hope that by explaining some of your legal rights you will know what to expect and understand what options you have.

You may well not need to read the whole book to solve your problem. The contents list at the beginning may indicate the chapter that is most relevant to your situation. The index at the end of the book may point you straight to the information you need. Finally, there is a list of agencies at the back of the book where you will be able to go to for more detailed advice.

Please note that the law applies to England and Wales only.

SHAC publishes a companion book to this guide for unmarried women experiencing relationship breakdown. *Going It Alone* is available directly from SHAC, 189a Old Brompton Road, London SW5 0AR, price £3.95.

chapter one

Using the Law

If you feel that your marriage is breaking down, or that you want to leave your husband, you may have to take legal action. You may need to sort out who is going to have the children, and where you are going to live. If your husband is violent, you may have to take legal action quickly. This chapter outlines how the law works.

You will probably need the help of a lawyer to sort out many of your problems. You may qualify for financial help (see Legal Aid, page 00) to pay for this. Even if you are receiving professional advice, it is important that you should understand what is happening, and that you should make the best choice for yourself.

How to approach the courts

This section deals with:

☐ how to get a solicitor;

☐ how to get Legal Aid;

☐ how the different courts work.

The legal profession has two branches. The lawyer you go to first will be a **solicitor**. A solicitor is a general practitioner in law. If your case is very complicated, or if it means going to court, your solicitor may decide to hire a **barrister**. A barrister is a lawyer who specialises in certain areas of the law, and is an expert at presenting cases in court. You can get Legal Aid to cover the cost of a barrister, as well as the cost of the solicitor (see Legal Aid, page 2).

Finding the right solicitor

Not all solicitors will be able to help. You will need one who:

☐ operates the Legal Aid Scheme;

☐ will do emergency work if necessary;

☐ specialises in family law.

If you were married abroad, or came here to marry your husband, you will need a solicitor who is also familiar with immigration and nationality law.

Finally you will need a solicitor who understands how you feel and who is willing to discuss your case with you.

Most libraries and Citizens Advice Bureaux have a **Legal Aid solicitors list**. This list has information about solicitors who operate the Legal Aid Scheme (see page 3). It also gives information about the work each solicitor does: (for example, family law, criminal law, etc), but you may have to phone several solicitors before you find one who is willing and able to take your case. Women's Aid refuges and advice centres will have experience of local solicitors whom they have found helpful. If your situation is complicated by the fact that you were married abroad, or came here to marry your husband you should contact **The Joint Council for the Welfare of Immigrants** or your local **Community Relations Council** to get in touch with a solicitor who is familiar with immigration and nationality law. For addresses see Appendix 1.

Not satisfied with your solicitor?

If you are unhappy with the way in which your solicitor is dealing with your case you can, in the last resort, change to another solicitor. The new solicitor may find it difficult to start any work until the old solicitor has passed all the papers over. There may be difficulties if the old solicitor is slow to act because, for example, s/he has not been paid by Legal Aid, although this should never be an excuse for delay.

Remember, it is you who are employing the solicitor. If you are unhappy about the way your case is going, or if you don't know what is happening, you have every right to ask for an explanation. A good solicitor is one who keeps you fully informed at all times.

Legal Aid

When you consult a solicitor, both you and the solicitor want to know how you are going to pay for the case. Never feel embarrassed to ask how much the case will cost. Ask to be assessed under the **Green Form** and **Legal Aid Scheme**. Even if you are not able to get all your costs paid, you may be entitled to some help. This would be cheaper than paying for the whole matter yourself.

Legal Aid is a scheme which gives you help with your legal costs. Not all solicitors operate the Legal Aid Scheme, so check with your local advice centres which solicitors do Legal Aid work in your area.

GREEN FORM SCHEME

The Green Form Scheme pays the solicitor to give you advice and assistance. It is called this because you will be asked to sign a green form. The solicitor is limited as to the type and amount of work s/he can do on this scheme. Usually, the solicitor can perform about two to three hours work. As the scheme is only for advice and assistance, your solicitor cannot represent you (that is, go to court with you) under this scheme. If your case is complicated, or has to go to court you will have to apply for full Legal Aid (see below). If you are on Income Support or Family Credit you will not be required to pay a contribution unless you have savings.

Even if you have savings, you may still not be required to pay anything. The amount of savings you can have before you have to pay varies according to the number of dependents you have. The rates are changed each year in April.

Otherwise your income will be assessed and you will have to pay a contribution. The assessment is based on your net income (after deduction of tax and national insurance) and any dependents you may have.

Your solicitor can tell you straight away how much you will be required to pay. If you are uncertain whether you can get Legal Aid on the Green Form Scheme, then many solicitors can give you an interview at a fixed fee of £5.00. To find out which local solicitors can do this, contact your local advice centre.

FULL LEGAL AID

If you need to be represented in court, or if there are disputes between you and your husband about property, maintenance or children, you will have to apply for full Legal Aid. The Legal Aid form is very complicated, and your solicitor can help you fill it in. S/he can charge for this (unless the work is done as part of your advice and assistance under the Green Form Scheme).

You will be sent a twelve-page financial statement to complete so that your means can be assessed. It is the Law Society, and not your solicitor who assesses your means. If you do not co-operate, you risk losing your Legal Aid and you will have to pay the costs yourself. If you are working, there will also be a form for your employer to fill in. It can take a long time, sometimes months, to get Legal Aid. Your solicitor will have to wait until s/he gets approval before s/he starts work, because s/he will not be paid for any work done before the **Legal Aid Certificate** (stating that you have got Legal Aid) is granted.

EMERGENCIES

In cases of emergency, for example, where a child has been snatched, your solicitor can get emergency Legal Aid immediately. This can be done over the telephone. You must then apply for full Legal Aid. If you do not, you will have to pay for the cost of the work done on the emergency certificate from the beginning.

If entitled, you are then made an offer of Legal Aid. You will be told how much (if any) your contributions will be — you can usually pay by instalments. These instalments are payable over a period of 12 months. The certificate will not be granted until you have accepted its terms. You must tell your solicitor of any changes in your financial circumstances (for example, maintenance) as this may affect your contributions. You must maintain your contributions, because if you do not, you risk losing your certificate.

STATUTORY CHARGE

If you are legally aided, this does not mean that you are getting your solicitor's services free. The Legal Aid Fund can put a **charge** on any capital or property you obtain in the proceedings. A charge is the right to claim back all the legal costs. This does not apply to the first £2,500 of any property, money or capital. This means that if you receive a lump sum payment or a share in any property, you will have to pay your legal costs out of it, but you will be able to keep the first £2,500. Your legal costs will come out of the rest. If the property is your home, and it is transferred into your name, you may not have to pay the legal costs immediately. The Law Society will have a charge registered against the property, so that if you sell it, you will have to pay the Law Society the costs of your case at the time of the sale.

Sometimes the Law Society will agree to transfer the charge to any new property so that the costs will not be paid until that new property is sold, but they don't have to agree to do this. Your solicitor should make clear to you the effect of a charge being placed on any settlement you are offered.

ADDITIONAL POINTS

You can cut your legal costs by:

☐ taking all relevant documents with you when you go to see a solicitor;

☐ giving your solicitor accurate and detailed information;

☐ listening carefully;

☐ keeping a running total of your costs. Every contact with your solicitor costs money.

Remember: the solicitor is taking your instructions on what you want for yourself and your children. However, the solicitor must tell the Law Society if s/he thinks that you are behaving unreasonably, for example, refusing an offer of settlement which your solicitor thinks is reasonable. If you are not happy with the advice you have had from your solicitor, ring an advice centre to talk it over.

Types of court

The next section describes the different kinds of courts you will come across. Which court you go to will be decided by what you need, for example, whether it is maintenance (money), custody of children, or a divorce.

MAGISTRATES' COURT

This court is used for:

☐ applying for child custody orders (see page 31);

☐ care proceedings taken by the local authority (see page 36);

☐ criminal prosecutions for assault or trespass (see page 9).

Magistrates' courts are usually quicker, but they don't have all the same powers as a county court (for example, they are limited in the amount of money that they can order your husband to pay as a lump sum). You should discuss your situation with your solicitor before starting any proceedings in the magistrates' court. It may be that the county court would be more suitable.

You cannot get a divorce or judicial separation in a magistrates' court.

A hearing in a magistrates' court can be a very unpleasant experience for the woman concerned, because of the way in which evidence is given. This must be verbal, and often means long and detailed accounts of any past violence and the whole history of the relationship.

JUVENILE COURT

This court is used for care proceedings taken by the local authority. It is made up of three magistrates, and the procedure is very similar to that of the magistrates' court.

COUNTY COURT

This court is used for:

☐ applying for an injunction (see page 7);

☐ applying for custody of children (see page 28);

☐ settling property – if you are living in owner-occupied property (see page 51).

If you are applying for a divorce, or judicial separation, you will have to go to a divorce county court. These deal with civil, not crimimal law and are therefore concerned with how to solve problems connected with the ending of the relationship, rather than whose 'fault' it is. The judge in a county court is a paid professional and will have more legal experience and qualifications than a lay magistrate. County courts can also provide wider and more long-term solutions (for example, they can make an order as to who shall have the matrimonial home). Where you have suffered violence or threats of violence, the powers of the county court are more extensive: for example, they can grant emergency orders, called injunctions, on your evidence alone, to get your husband to leave the matrimonial home (see Chapter 2).

HIGH COURT

This court is used for:

☐ applying to make a child a ward of court (see pages 32 and 37);

☐ appealing against decisions made in other courts.

If your solicitor disagrees with a decision made in another court (for example, a county court) regarding money, custody or property, s/he can appeal against that decision in the High Court. Appeals are rare and cannot be made just because the court has decided against you. Your solicitor will have to show that the original decision was wrong in law and that you have a strong chance of winning. Also, if your divorce is defended (if your husband does not want a divorce but you do), your case will be transferred to the High Court. If your case goes to the High Court, you will have to be represented by a barrister.

chapter two

Violence and immediate housing options

If your husband has been violent or has threatened violence to you or your children, you may want to leave your home, at least temporarily, or get your husband to leave. There are various things you could do:

☐ apply for an injunction to get your husband out of the home;

☐ go to stay with friends or relatives;

☐ go to a Women's Aid refuge;

☐ go to the council for help.

These will be dealt with in turn.

Important Note: **If you do leave home in an emergency never give up your tenancy. The council may decide that by giving up your tenancy you have made yourself 'intentionally homeless' and they will not, therefore, be legally obliged to rehouse you (see page 17).**

Injunctions

If your husband has been violent or has threatened violence to you or your children, you can apply for an order from the court to restrain him, or get him to leave. If there is no violence, but you feel that your husband's behaviour is so bad that it is disturbing you or the children, you may also be able to apply for an injunction to get him to leave. You may want to stay with friends, or go to a Women's Aid refuge (see page 13) while you do this.

An injunction is a written order from the court which can tell your husband to do one or more things. It is important that you tell your solicitor the full story so s/he knows what to ask the court to put on the injunction. The order can tell him:

☐ Not to assault you, molest you, or harass you. This includes physical assault, threats, or verbal abuse, or anything which stops you going about your daily routine.

☐ Not to allow his friends, relatives or any other person to assault, molest or harass you.

☐ Not to assault your children (under 18), or any children living with you, and to restrain his friends from doing the same.

☐ To leave the home, and not to return (this is called an 'ouster' or 'exclusion' order).

☐ To keep a certain distance from your home or any other place where you go regularly, for example, your place of work.

☐ To let you back into the home.

☐ The court can make arrangements for the children in an injunction if there have been problems.

☐ Not to damage, destroy or remove any of your property from your home.

Types of injunction

When you go to a solicitor to try to get an injunction to protect yourself, there are many ways in which s/he can help you. The type of injunction will depend upon your individual needs, and circumstances. Your solicitor can advise you which is the best way for you.

As part of custody proceedings
If you are married, but you have not started proceedings for divorce or judicial separation, and there is a dispute about who is to have the children: an application for an injunction can be made as part of proceedings to obtain custody of your children under the **Guardianship of Minors Act 1971**.

As part of divorce proceedings
If you are married, and you have not begun proceedings for divorce or

judicial separation, and there is no dispute about the custody of the children: you can get an injunction in a magistrates' court under the **Domestic Proceedings and Magistrates' Court Act 1978**, or you can apply for an injunction in a county court under the **Domestic Violence and Matrimonial Proceedings Act 1976**.

If you are married, and you wish to start proceedings for divorce or judicial separation: you can get an injunction as part of those proceedings; you do not have to start separate proceedings for an injunction.

As part of proceedings for assault or trespass
If you have already obtained a divorce, and your ex-husband is still violent to you or keeps coming round to your home when you don't want him there: you will have to take action against your husband in the county court for **assault**. (This means violence, or threats of violence.) If he just keeps coming in to your home, you can take action against him for **trespassing** on your property.

How to get an injunction

Once you and your solicitor have decided which court you are going to use, the next step is actually what happens in court.

The hearing will be in chambers (that means the public will be excluded). If you decide to use the county court, your solicitor will have to produce an affidavit (that is, a sworn statement) of your evidence which will include such matters as:

☐ how many children you have;

☐ what accommodation is available to you;

☐ what accommodation is available to your husband;

☐ details of your husband's conduct;

☐ why you need the injunction.

If you do not want your husband to know where you are, you can ask the court if you can keep your address secret.

Generally, the court will look at the following matters when deciding whether to give you your injunction. The criteria may vary according to which Act and which court you use; but here are the most important factors:

☐ **Conduct:** violence, of course, is relevant, but if there is no violence you may still get an exclusion order. Other behaviour is also taken into account. You must include details of your husband's conduct in your sworn statement (affidavit).

- [ ] **Needs and Resources:** this means that the court will look at where you are living and whether it is adequate for you and the children, and where your husband could live if he had to leave the home.

- [ ] **Needs of any children:** the court will have the welfare of the children very much in mind, so if the children are upset by the behaviour of your husband, you are more likely to get an exclusion or ouster order. However, this also means that if your children have a particularly good relationship with their father, and he has been violent or threatening only to you, they may decide that the best thing for the children is for their father to be at home with them.

- [ ] **All circumstances of the case:** the court will consider these factors one by one, and then attempt to decide on the right thing to do in the circumstances.

It is easier to obtain a non-molestation order than an ouster or exclusion order.

If your solicitor decides to apply for an injunction in the magistrates' court, s/he will use the **Domestic Proceedings and Magistrates' Court Act 1978**. You cannot get the same range of injunctions in the magistrates' court as in the county court. The differences are:

- [ ] An injunction which divides up the home between you, and excludes your husband from just part of the home is not obtainable in the magistrates' court.

- [ ] An order which forbids him to come within a certain area of the home is not obtainable in the magistrates' court.

- [ ] There must have been actual violence before an exclusion order is granted by the magistrates' court. This is not essential in the county court.

- [ ] Injunctions in the magistrates' courts have different names – an injunction telling your husband not to be violent towards you or the children is called a **'personal protection order'**.

Evidence of violence

Evidence of violence is not always essential in order to get an ouster injunction in a county court. If your children are suffering emotionally, or are at risk, this may be sufficient to get you an ouster order in a county court. For legal action, it is a good idea to have proof from a professional person if you can. If your husband assaults you, even if you don't need treatment, you should go to your **doctor** and ask him/her to put what has happened on record. If you prefer you can go to the **casualty department** of your local hospital. The staff there should record what injuries you have, and should notify your doctor. If you feel easier talking to a **social worker** or **health visitor**, then do that. If you can't get confirmation of violence from a professional, then a friend's evidence is better than none at all. If there are no witnesses, or other evidence, don't worry. You will have a chance of putting your story to the court in your affidavit or in person, and that may be sufficient.

Urgent cases

Normally your solicitor will have to give your husband four days' notice of an application for an injunction. However, if you need an injunction urgently, it is possible to go to court without giving your husband any notice – this is called an *ex parte* hearing. You can get emergency Legal Aid for this. You can only get an ouster, or exclusion injunction under this procedure in cases of exceptional violence or danger. Any order granted under this procedure will usually only last seven days, and your solicitor will have to serve notice on your husband in the normal way to get a longer ouster or exclusion order. It is particularly difficult to get a 'power of arrest' attached to an *ex parte* order. You will never have to serve the order on your husband yourself. Your solicitor can employ a person specially (called a **process server**) who will do this for you.

If the *ex parte* is not granted your solicitor will have to serve notice on your husband in the usual way.

If you need an emergency injunction at a time when the courts are closed, for example, at a weekend, you are still entitled to have a judge hear your case. Your solicitor will need to telephone the High Court, if you are in London, or the local police station in other areas to get details of the duty judge.

If the injunction is disobeyed

If your husband does not obey the injunction, he has disobeyed the court. He can then be brought back to court, and the judge can either alter the terms of the injunction to try to make it more effective, or s/he can imprison your husband for **'contempt of court'**. The judge is unlikely to do this unless s/he considers your case to be very serious. If your husband promises to behave well in the future, the judge will probably accept his word, and only give him a warning. If your husband does go to prison it is likely to be only for a very short time (until he is considered to have 'purged his contempt' – that is, until he has apologised sufficiently to the court).

A more effective way of getting your husband to obey an injunction is to get a 'power of arrest' attached.

Power of arrest

You can get a power of arrest attached to some injunctions. This means if your husband breaks the injunction, the police can arrest him without a warrant. A power of arrest can only be attached if:

☐ there has been actual bodily harm; and

☐ there is a likelihood of future violence.

Some judges are reluctant to attach a power of arrest. You may have to be very persistent to ensure that a power of arrest is attached to your injunction.

If you do get a power of arrest, take a copy down to the local police station so that they know about your situation. Unfortunately, you cannot be sure that the police will help you if your husband does break the terms of the order. They have a long tradition of not getting involved with domestic disputes. A power of arrest only means that they *can* arrest your husband, not that they will. Some police stations are more sympathetic than others.

If you have no power of arrest attached to your injunction, and your husband does not obey it, you will have to return to court to ask for your husband to be committed to prison.

If you think that taking out an injunction would just make things worse and put you or your children in more danger, don't be forced into doing this. If the council is pressurising you to start injunction proceedings, ring a local advice centre or Women's Aid refuge.

Staying with friends and relatives

If your husband has been violent, and you are frightened and upset you may decide to go and stay with friends or relatives. Often these seem to be the easiest people to turn to, especially if you have already talked to them about what has been going on. You won't have to tell everything to strangers. Your children will probably already know your friends or relatives, and this will be a big help.

Staying with friends and relatives need not affect your long-term rights to your home (see page 44), but may solve your immediate difficulties. However, there are likely to be problems. Your husband probably knows who your friends and relatives are. If you are escaping a violent husband it might be better to go somewhere he can't find you. Also, you are likely to be overcrowded. It may take a long time to sort out your problems. Can you be sure that they can keep you for any length of time?

Alternatively, it may be possible to find a Women's Aid refuge (see page 14).

Staying in a Women's Aid refuge

There are now around 150 Women's Aid refuges throughout the country. They are for women who need a safe place to stay because the person they live with has been violent. It doesn't matter whether you have children or not. In an emergency, the police have the telephone number of your local refuge, and they can escort you there, if it is necessary.

What is a refuge?

A refuge is a house, usually with a secret address, which provides a temporary home to women who have suffered violence. You will meet women there who have been through similar experiences. You can get advice there on how to claim benefits, how to get a good solicitor and how to apply to the council for housing. The houses are run by the women who live in them (there is no warden). The women who work there will have had lots of contact with local agencies and will have information about the local homeless persons unit at the council, the Department of Social Security office, schools, social workers, doctors and solicitors. Going from one office to another can be an unpleasant experience, and it is best to know as much as you can about what you will have to go through. There may be someone at the refuge who can accompany you.

Refuges vary a lot. Some have been set up by councils and are run by social workers, employed by the council. Most Women's Aid refuges were set up by a group of women who still support the people living and working in the refuge. Their aims are:

☐ to provide a safe place on request for women and their children who have suffered physical or mental violence;

☐ to offer support and advice to any woman who needs it, whether or not she lives in the refuge;

☐ to offer support to women and their children after they have left the refuge.

DISADVANTAGES

The main problem about refuges is that they are very busy. They can be difficult places to live in, because it is likely that you will have to live in overcrowded conditions for some time. You will have to share kitchen and washing facilities with a lot of other women and children. There is little privacy and you may find it difficult to adapt after living in an ordinary family home.

How to find a refuge

To protect the women who stay there, refuges don't advertise their addresses. You can get the telephone numbers of refuges from the Women's Aid Federation (see Useful Addresses, Appendix 1).

Individual refuges are very often full and have to close their doors. However, they will always give you the telephone number of a refuge close by where there will be space. They promise that no woman is ever turned away. You don't have to go to the refuge near your present home. If you want to get a long way away from your husband, tell them that, and they will try to fit you in.

You can also get the number of a refuge from:

☐ a local advice centre;

☐ social services at the council;

☐ the police.

Help from the council

If you want to leave your home now because of violence or threats of violence, and don't want to return to the matrimonial home at a later date, you can make an application to the council as a homeless person. The **Housing Act 1985 Part III** gives councils a duty to help women who have suffered violence or threats of violence from someone in the same house as them. But you also have to be in **priority need** before you will get temporary accommodation (see page 16).

If you are not British and came to the UK to marry your husband, or if there are any conditions attached to your stay, for example, that you should not have recourse to public funds (such as welfare benefits), then contact the Joint Council for the Welfare of Immigrants for advice before you approach any local council. Your application for housing may affect your right to stay in this country (see Useful Addresses, Appendix 1).

The Housing Act 1985 Part III places duties on the councils and they must follow it. They have no choice. There is also a Code of Guidance which

14

tells councils how they should interpret certain parts of the Act. The Code of Guidance is not law – the council only has to consider its recommendations. This means that one council could treat you quite differently from another council.

There are two main ways for you to get council housing: by the waiting list, or by applying for emergency help if you are homeless.

The waiting list is for people who need housing in the area but who are not homeless. They will be assessed by the council and will have to wait for a home to be offered to them. How long they wait depends on a number of things such as the size of accommodation they require, and what conditions they have to live in now. Often people have to wait for a very long time.

If your husband is violent to you, then the council should not treat you as a waiting list applicant. They should look at your application under the terms of the Housing Act 1985 Part III.

Some councils have a separate department or office for people who are homeless called the **homeless persons unit** or **emergency housing office**. Try to make sure that you are seen by the right department, or your application could be delayed.

You can ask any council to help you if you are homeless. It does not have to be the council where you live. If you are too frightened to go to the local council, you can go to one in another area.

You can find the address of the homeless persons unit by ringing the council. It will be in the telephone book, or ask an advice centre, or the police.

All councils have to have a 24-hour emergency service. If you need to leave in a hurry at night, or at the weekend, phone the police to find out what the emergency arrangements in your area are.

The homeless persons unit

You will be interviewed by an officer from the homeless persons unit. It can be an upsetting interview, because they will need to take details of how you came to be homeless. It is a good idea to take a friend with you if you can. Make a note of the name of the person who interviewed you as you may need to speak to him/her again. Take a note of anything that s/he asks you to do, or any documents that s/he says s/he needs to see.

You will probably be asked to sign a statement saying that everything you have told them is true.

When the council interview you they are trying to find out four main things:

☐ Are you homeless?

☐ Are you in priority need?

☐ Have you made yourself homeless?

☐ Do you have a local connection?

The next section explains what these terms mean, and what the council are looking for. This is a brief description of what the Act says. If you are not happy with the treatment you receive, see page 19.

ARE YOU HOMELESS?

The council will first look into whether they think that you are homeless. They must accept that you are homeless if you are suffering violence, or threats of violence from someone who is likely to carry them out, and who lives in the same house as you. In practice, some councils will insist that you must have suffered violence. This is not correct. If you have suffered threats of violence, you should be accepted as homeless. However, if you are suffering violence from someone who does not live with you, then you are not homeless according to the Act. You are also homeless if there is nowhere that you are legally entitled to live.

ARE YOU IN PRIORITY NEED?

The council must accept that you are in priority need if:

☐ you have children under 16;

☐ you have children who are under 19 and who are in full time education or training. Take your children's birth certificates with you to the interview at the homeless persons unit;

☐ you are pregnant. Take along confirmation of your pregnancy to your interview with the homeless persons officer;

☐ you are over 60. Take proof of your age with you;

☐ you become homeless because of a flood, fire or other disaster;

☐ you are vulnerable by reason of physical or mental disability, or other special reason. Take any proof, such as a doctor's letter, with you when you go to the homeless persons unit. The council makes the decision whether or not to treat you as vulnerable but they should accept you if:

■ you are registered disabled with the local social services department;

- you are mentally ill or handicapped (you will need evidence from your doctor or psychiatrist);

- you are approaching retirement age and are in poor health.

Some councils will also accept as vulnerable:

☐ single battered women at risk of further violence if they return home, or at risk of violent pursuit;

☐ young women at risk (usually teenagers).

If the council have reason to believe that you *may* be homeless and in priority need, they have a duty to provide you with temporary accommodation, straight away. These things should be established in the first interview so that you can have temporary accommodation the same night. If you have problems getting temporary accommodation, get in touch with an advice centre immediately. The council can complete their enquiries into the other things that concern them later.

DID YOU MAKE YOURSELF HOMELESS?

Councils do not have to provide permanent housing for people who have made themselves homeless. These people, the Act calls **'intentionally homeless'**.

The Act says that you are intentionally homeless if:

☐ you deliberately did something or failed to do something, the result of which was your becoming homeless;

☐ the accommodation you lost was reasonable for you to live in. When looking at whether it was reasonable for you to live there, the council can look at other housing needs in their area.

The Code of Guidance says "A battered woman who has fled the home should never be regarded as having become homeless intentionally because it clearly would not be reasonable for her to remain".

DO YOU HAVE A LOCAL CONNECTION?

The council will look into whether you have a local connection with their area. Women who have suffered violence cannot be referred back to the area where they might be at risk of violence.

You have a local connection with an area if:

☐ **Residence:** you have lived in the area for six months out of the last twelve, or three years out of the last five years.

☐ **Employment:** you or any member of your immediate family has a permanent job in the area.

- [ ] **Family associations:** if you have close family connections in the area, you may have a local connection. This might be if you have parents, brothers or sisters, or grown-up children who have lived in the area for at least five years.

- [ ] **Special circumstances:** if you have a special reason for wanting to live in the area, such as a local community who speak your language, you can try to argue that these are special circumstances that give you a 'local connection'.

If you have *no* local connection with the council in the area you have applied to, don't worry. They still have a duty to look at your case, and to make a decision.

If the council think that you are homeless, and in priority need, they have a duty to find you somewhere to go immediately. This may be **temporary accommodation**. They have to provide you with temporary accommodation if they have **'reason to believe that you may be homeless'**. You do not have to *prove* that you are homeless, and in priority need – just that you *may* be homeless and in priority need. If the council do not offer you temporary accommodation, contact your local advice centre straight away.

Temporary accommodation

There are several sorts of ways in which the council can provide temporary accommodation:

- [ ] If you have been staying with friends or relatives, the council may ring them up and ask them if you can stay with them a bit longer. If your friends or relatives *don't* want you to stay then ask them to make this clear to the council. If they are happy for you to stay for a short time, then make sure the council knows this, and the exact date when you are going to have to leave. Ask your friends to put this in writing. The council must continue to investigate your case, even if you can stay temporarily with friends or relatives. The council may try to argue that your friends need to get a court order to evict you. This is wrong in law. If you moved in as a friendly arrangement, it is likely that you will be a **licensee**, and your friends can evict you after giving you **reasonable notice**. When the notice has expired, you should present yourself at the homeless persons unit and ask to be provided with temporary accommodation straight away.

- [ ] The council may ring a refuge and ask them to take you in (see page 13 for an explanation of what refuges are). While you are in a refuge, the council should accept that you are homeless.

- The council may find a place for you in one of their own hostels. These are usually run by the council and may have a warden living on the premises. The standard of accommodation varies a lot. Often families have to share facilities such as kitchens, bathrooms and laundries.

- The council may find you a room in a **bed and breakfast hotel**. Many councils in London put families into hotels while looking into their cases. They vary in size, facilities, rules and regulations. You probably will be very overcrowded, and have to share facilities with other families. Many hotels do not have kitchens so you may have to eat out which is very expensive. Some hotels have a rule which says that you have to be out of your room for a number of hours each day.

- **Mother and baby homes**. If you are young, living alone and expecting your first child, the council may decide to place you in a mother and baby home. There is usually a matron who is resident and who looks after the home. S/he is concerned with the welfare of the people living in the home. The home places a lot of emphasis on ante-natal and post-natal care. You may be expected to help with the housework, although most of the cooking and other work will be done by staff employed at the home. The afternoons are free for visitors, and there is usually a visitors' room. What the home is like will depend a lot on the matron – but they are intended to be friendly and helpful places.

- **Short-life housing schemes**. These make use of old houses which the council intend to improve or demolish later. They are usually in rather poor repair. You are most likely to be moved to short-life housing after some weeks in other temporary accommodation (e.g. in bed and breakfast). The advantage of this type of accommodation is that you will have your own front door and you can have your own furniture with you. The main disadvantage is that it may be in poor repair. It must still be wind and weather proof. If you think that your accommodation doesn't even meet this standard, ring your local advice centre.

The council may arrange for a social worker to visit you while you are in temporary accommodation to talk to you about your problems. You can also ring a Women's Aid refuge for advice if you left home because of violence.

Challenging the council's decision

If you do not like the decision that the council makes, insist on a copy in writing.

The law on homelessness is very complex and any decision that the council makes may give grounds for challenge. **It is essential that you obtain expert advice from a housing aid centre, Citizens Advice Bureau or law centre before trying to challenge the council.**

These are some of the decisions that the council may make, and some ways to argue with them.

YOU ARE NOT HOMELESS BECAUSE YOU CAN GO BACK TO YOUR HUSBAND

This can only be true if you and your husband have lived together in the home. If your husband has acquired the home since you separated, and you have never lived there, you will have no right to live in it.

If your husband has been violent, or has threatened violence, then the council cannot say that you are not homeless.

If the council does not accept that there has been violence, produce proof of the violence, if you can, from a doctor or social worker or from hospital or police records. If you do not have this kind of proof, ask any of your friends or relatives who have seen your husband's violence to act as a witness. If there has never been any witnesses, then point out that you have signed a statement declaring everything you say is true, and that they must believe you unless they have good cause to believe that you are not telling the truth. If your husband has been violent to someone else, and there is proof of this (e.g. he has a violent criminal record) this can be evidence that he is likely to carry out any threats of violence that he has made to you.

YOU ARE NOT IN PRIORITY NEED

If you have left your children with relatives while you sort out your problems, the council may try to say that you are not in priority need.

The Code of Guidance says that if you have children, even if they are not living with you, you should be considered as being in priority need.

If your children are in care, the council may try to say that you are not in priority need.

If your children have been in voluntary care for less than six months, you may take them away without giving the council notice. You should point this out to the council and they should accept that you are in priority need. If your children are subject to a care order, then the council should consult the children's social worker in order to decide whether you are in priority need. If it is reasonable to expect them to live with you, you should be considered as in priority need.

20

If you haven't got any children, the council may try to say that you are not in priority need.

> If you are over 60 you should be treated as being in priority need. If you are in poor health, registered disabled, or recently discharged from a mental institution you should point this out to the council, and ask them to assess you as 'vulnerable', and therefore in need of housing. Some councils accept that if you are at risk of further violence if you return home, or if you are at risk of violent pursuit, you should be accepted as in priority need. If this is your case, draw this to the attention of the council staff and ask them why they are not accepting you as in priority need. In addition, if you are a young woman at risk of sexual or financial exploitation, you should ask the council to treat you as in priority need.

YOU SHOULD GET AN INJUNCTION TO GET YOUR HUSBAND TO LEAVE THE HOME

Councils may advise you to get an injunction to get your husband out of the home so that you can go back there. They may say that you will then be safe and that you will not suffer from violence.

☐ Even if you do apply for one, an injunction will take time to obtain, and the council should give you temporary accommodation until this happens.

☐ If you feel that your husband would not obey an injunction, or would become more violent, you can point this out. If your husband has broken previous injunctions you should give the council details.

☐ You may not get an 'ouster' injunction (see page 8), even if there is violence, for example, if you do not want to return home. If your solicitor feels that this is the case and that it is not worthwhile applying for an injunction, ask him/her to put this in writing and take a copy to the council.

The council may say that you will be 'intentionally homeless' if you don't follow their advice. If they do not accept your arguments contact a local advice centre before taking action.

YOU HAVE NO LOCAL CONNECTION WITH THE AREA TO WHICH YOU HAVE APPLIED

If this is the case, the council is entitled to 'refer' you back to an area where you do have a local connection for rehousing.

> Even if you have no local connection with the area where you have applied, the council must still provide temporary accommodation for you. If they intend to 'refer' or to send you to another area for rehousing, they

must tell you so in writing. They must also show that you *do* have a local connection in that area. They must not refer you to an area where you have suffered or are likely to suffer violence.

What must the council do for you?

The council have several duties to people who make applications to them under the **Housing Act 1985 Part III**.

Decision in writing

One of the most useful parts of the Act is Section 64 which says that whatever decision the council make, they must put that decision in writing. If you do not like the council's decision, then ask for your **Section 64 Notice**. If you wish to dispute the council's decision contact your local advice centre. You must do this straight away, because there is a time limit of three months within which you can challenge a council's decision.

Advice and assistance

They must give you advice and assistance. If you are homeless, but you are not in priority need, the council have a duty to give you advice and assistance to help you to find somewhere to live. However, this is often nothing but a list of local hotels.

Temporary accommodation

If you are homeless and in priority need, the council must give you temporary accommodation until they have finished their enquiries. If they decide that you are intentionally homeless (see page 17) then they must give you a period of time in temporary accommodation to help you to try and find somewhere on your own. If the council decide that you are intentionally homeless then they must also give you advice and assistance as well. Again, this is often just a list of local hotels.

Rehousing

If the council decides that they must house you permanently they must ensure that you have temporary accommodation until they are able to make you an offer. The council will probably make you an offer of council housing (although they can arrange for you to get housing from someone else). They have a duty to make you an offer of reasonable accommodation. In some areas, councils only make *one* offer of accommodation. If you do not like the offer of housing that you have been made, do *not* refuse it straight away. It is very difficult to dispute offers of housing that are made. Only if the place is in very poor condition or if it is impossible for you to get to work from that place will you have a chance of disputing the offer. If you want to refuse an offer of housing, *get advice straight away.*

Storing furniture

If the council have a duty to provide accommodation for you, whether it is permanent or temporary, they must also take steps to make sure that your property does not become damaged or lost. The council usually takes it into storage. They are allowed to make a reasonable charge. The council are not allowed to get rid of it unless:

- [ ] you can now look after it yourself;

- [ ] they believe you have abandoned it. If this is the case, they must write to you at your last known address, and let you have a chance to recover it.

If you have furniture in store with the council you should:

- [ ] make an **inventory** (a list) of what you have put there;

- [ ] make sure the council know your address, so that they can write to you;

- [ ] when the furniture is delivered to you, check every item against the inventory. Do not sign anything to say that you have received furniture which is missing.

If there is any dispute about the ownership of the property, or if you fear that your husband may damage property which belongs to you, get legal advice. You can take action in the county court to decide the ownership of it, and to prevent your husband disposing of it. If your husband has already sold it, or got rid of it, you can get compensation.

chapter three

Divorce and judicial separation

If your relationship with your husband is breaking down, you may be considering whether you want to end your marriage by getting a **divorce** or formally separate by getting a **judicial separation**.

The procedure for divorce has become very much easier recently, especially in the case of **undefended divorces**, where you and your husband agree to get a divorce. There are still some things that may stop you from getting a divorce straight away. You cannot get a divorce in the first year of your marriage. You still need to prove that your marriage has broken down. You can only do this on one of the following grounds. The list assumes that you are the one who wants to get a divorce, but of course either you or your husband can petition for divorce.

Adultery

It is very difficult to prove adultery unless your husband is prepared to sign a confession statement. It is very unlikely that you will get Legal Aid to cover the cost of an **enquiry agent** (a person employed to get evidence of your husband's adultery). It is not just your husband's adultery that gives you the ground for divorce, you must also find it intolerable to live with him.

If, after your husband commits adultery, you decide that you want to try and 'rescue' the marriage you can still use his act of adultery as a basis for the divorce as long as you have not lived together since then for more than six months. If you decide during this period that it is intolerable for you to live with your husband, then you can still use the fact of his adultery to petition for divorce. If you live together for more than six months after you have discovered the adultery, then it can be said that you have not found it intolerable to live with your husband and that, in effect, you have forgiven him.

Unreasonable behaviour

Unreasonable behaviour can include violence or mental cruelty.

If you decide to try and live together after you have alleged unreasonable behaviour, you can still rely on this ground to get your divorce as long as you have not lived with him for more than six months since. If you have lived with him for more than six months, it is assumed that you have forgiven him, that you can be reasonably expected to live with him, and that you are no longer entitled to a divorce on the basis of his original unreasonable behaviour.

Desertion

To seek a divorce on this ground, you have to show that your husband intended to desert you, and that there is no good reason why you should live apart (for example, he must not be apart from you just because he is in hospital, or in prison). You must also be able to say that you have always wanted your husband to return, and that you never did anything to cause him to leave. You can be deserted even if you continue to live in the same house. If your husband withdraws into one or two rooms, and stops having anything to do with you, you can claim to have been deserted. Any sharing that you do, such as eating meals together or sharing a living room would mean that in effect you have not been deserted. If you attempt to rescue your marriage during this period, the court can ignore any period or periods that you lived together as long as they don't add up to more than six months. You must have been deserted for two years in all to get a divorce on this ground, not including any period of reconciliation.

Separation

You can prove that your marriage has broken down simply because you have lived apart for a period of time. For divorce on the grounds of separation alone, you can only apply for a divorce once the two-year period (with consent) or five-year period (without consent) is over. If you try to 'rescue' your marriage during a period of separation, the court can disregard any time that you lived together, as long as the periods do not add up to more than six months. You can be living apart in the same house but you must have had separate households. Any sharing of living accommodation, meals, etc., will mean that you are not separated.

How do you get a divorce?

If your application for a divorce is undefended, there is a special procedure in the divorce court, which means that you will not have to give evidence or be present. It is still best to get the advice of a solicitor even if your husband does not intend to defend the divorce. You cannot get Legal Aid to be represented in an undefended divorce case. If there are other things to be sorted out, such as maintenance, custody of the children, or rights to the house, your solicitor can get Legal Aid separately for these matters.

When you go to a solicitor, you will need to complete a form, called a **'petition'** for divorce. Copies must be sent to your husband and, if you are alleging adultery, to the woman whom you name as the co-respondent (that is, the woman with whom you allege your husband committed adultery). You will have to sign a sworn statement, called an affidavit, giving the facts surrounding your request for a divorce.

When you go to your solicitor, take your marriage certificate or a certified copy. You can get this from the General Register Office (see Useful Addresses, Appendix 1). There is a charge. You will also have to make a statement of the proposed arrangements for any children of the marriage, because a **decree absolute** (that is, the final stage of the divorce) will not be granted unless the court is satisfied about the arrangements for the children.

When the papers are given to the court, the registrar will examine them. Copies will be sent to your husband, who will be given time to answer your petition. If the registrar is satisfied that you have grounds for a divorce, s/he will give directions that the case may go ahead to the next stage: the decree nisi. If there is anything that s/he is not happy about s/he may ask for further information. If you go ahead to the decree nisi, then the registrar will make an appointment for you to see the judge to discuss the arrangements for the children (see Chapter 4). This appointment is very often on the same day as the decree nisi.

DECREE NISI & DECREE ABSOLUTE

A **decree nisi** is a provisional declaration. It doesn't end the marriage. It just means that you can apply to end the marriage (to obtain a decree absolute) after six weeks have passed. After the decree absolute, the marriage is ended. A certificate will be sent to you from the court. You will need this if you want to get married again.

Defended divorce

Over ninety per cent of divorces are undefended. Even if you disagree about the custody of the children, or how much maintenance you should get, then it can still go ahead as an undefended divorce. The reason for this is that the courts now try to end marriages that have completely broken down as quickly and as painlessly as possible. The hearings about custody and maintenance will be separate.

If you are one of the few who are facing a defended divorce, your husband must fill out a form called an **'answer'** to your petition. This has to be done quickly. The registrar will make an appointment to see you both, and will try to see if there is any way that you can avoid a defended divorce. If there is not, then the registrar will make directions for a hearing in an open court. You will need a solicitor to represent you, and may need a barrister too. You can get Legal Aid if your divorce is defended.

Your husband may tell you when he first gets your petition for divorce that he intends to defend it. He may change his mind after he goes to a solicitor. The Law Society is very strict about the way in which it grants Legal Aid for defending a divorce.

Judicial separation

There is an alternative to getting a divorce, called **judicial separation**. A judicial separation means you are no longer bound to live together with your husband. It is a formal recognition of separation but does not end your marriage. You will not be free to remarry after a judicial separation.

If you don't want to start divorce proceedings straight away, or if you have religious objections to getting a divorce, a judicial separation might be best for you. You can get injunctions, custody orders, maintenance and property settlements as part of a judicial separation.

The method of getting a judicial separation is the same as that of getting a divorce as described above, except that there is only one decree and that is a final one.

chapter four

Children and custody

While you are married, both you and your husband have custody of your children and you both have **'parental rights'**. If you decide to get divorced, you cannot get a **decree absolute** (that is, the final stage of your divorce) unless the court is satisfied about the arrangements you have made for any children of the family. So when there are children involved, the court will always consider arrangements for custody, access and maintenance of the children. You may have to sort out problems such as, where the children are to live; or how much maintenance your husband should pay to support them.

You can apply for custody before divorce. This is called **'interim' custody**. Below are definitions of some of the legal terms which are used:

Parental Rights and Duties. These are responsibilities which married parents share. They include such things as:

☐ The right to have your children with you, and to make decisions about them.

☐ The right to choose their religion.

☐ The right to choose their education.

☐ The duty to see that the children go to school.

☐ The right to consent to a child's marriage while the child is under 18.

☐ The right of a parent to consent to medical treatment for a child.

Legal Custody. This is the right to make decisions about the child. This can be given to someone who doesn't actually have the child living with them.

Care and Control. This is the right to have the child living with you.

Access. The right to see your child.

'Children of the Marriage'. This means any children treated as family by both of you. This can include adopted children, step-children, foster children as well as your own children.

Arrangements for the children

If you are going through an undefended divorce, there is a special speedy procedure which means that a decree nisi will be granted without a hearing in court and you will not have to give evidence.

However, if you have children, you cannot get a decree absolute (the final stage), unless the court is satisfied about the arrangements for the future of any children of the marriage.

When deciding whether the arrangements for the children are satisfactory, the court will look at:

☐ **Residence.** Where will the children live? Whom will they live with? Who will look after them? Has that person agreed to look after them?

☐ **Education or training.** You will have to give the name and addresses of the places where the children are going to school or attending courses.

☐ **Financial arrangements.** Who is going to support them? Who is contributing the money? The court will look to see if there is enough money for their support.

☐ **Access.** What arrangements for access have been made? Are these good enough?

☐ **Disabilities.** The court will want to know about any disabilities that your children have, and whether they are receiving proper care.

☐ **Care orders.** The court will want to know about any care orders that have been made relating to your children (see Chapter 5).

In the case of undefended divorce, the court will make a special appointment in **chambers** (that is, in private) if there are children involved. Usually, the judge will be satisfied if you and your husband have agreed on all these matters.

Other things the judge can do

If you haven't agreed about the children or if the judge is not happy about the proposed arrangements, s/he can do any of these things:

Put off the hearing and ask for a report from the court welfare office:
A **court welfare officer** is an independent person who will interview you and your husband, look at reports from any doctor, teacher, social worker or probation officer involved, and will interview the children. The report will usually make a recommendation but the judge doesn't have to follow that recommendation.

Put off the hearing and appoint a guardian ad litem:
Sometimes (but quite rarely) the judge thinks that the child needs to be represented separately from you and your husband. The judge can appoint someone, usually from the **Official Solicitor's Office**, to act on behalf of the child. This person is called a *'guardian ad litem'*. The *guardian ad litem* has powers to investigate the facts fully, and to make a report to the court.

Ask you to attend a Conciliation Appointment
If there are difficulties about the children, some courts operate a **Conciliation Service**. This means that you both will be invited to attend an informal hearing in the registrar's room to try and sort things out. A court welfare officer will also be present. Children over the age of nine can also attend.

Orders about custody that the court may make

CUSTODY TO YOU, ACCESS TO YOUR HUSBAND
This is the most common type of arrangement. Access is often just called **'reasonable access'** and it is left to you to agree how this will be arranged. If you have special reasons for wanting it, you can ask for access to be spelt out. If you think that the children should only meet their father away from home or when supervised by a social worker, these conditions can be stated in the order.

CUSTODY TO BOTH YOU AND YOUR HUSBAND JOINTLY, 'CARE AND CONTROL' TO YOU
This means that you will have the child with you, but your husband has the right to be consulted about important decisions affecting the child. This type of decision is becoming more popular.

CUSTODY TO YOUR HUSBAND, 'CARE AND CONTROL' TO YOU
This means you will physically have the child, but your husband has the right to make important decisions about the child's life. These orders are very rare.

CUSTODY TO SOMEONE ELSE

It is possible for the court to grant custody to someone else especially where a child has been happily settled with them (for example, with a grandparent). This is rare.

Factors involved in this decision

The judge always puts the child's welfare first. But there can be differing ideas about what's best for a child. These are some of the things that will be considered:

- [ ] **The parents' wishes.**

- [ ] **The parents' conduct.** For example, if the children's father is violent to them he is less likely to get access. The court doesn't 'punish' people for bad conduct by taking children away from them, but sometimes they consider that a child's welfare might be affected by what they see as **'misconduct'**. For example, there have been cases where lesbian mothers have lost custody of their children.

- [ ] **The age and sex of the children.** The younger the children are, the more likely the court will grant the mother custody. If the children are older, custody of girls is often given to mothers and custody of older boys is given to fathers.

- [ ] **The wishes of the child.** If the court welfare officer interviews your child, the views of children over seven are usually taken into account.

- [ ] **Education and religion.** The child's future education prospects with either parent will be looked at.

- [ ] **Material advantages.** The material advantages that the child would have with one parent rather than another are not considered to be so important as his/her general welfare. The most important thing very often is **stability**. Courts do not like upsetting the stable homes or relationships that the child has already developed. If you have had the children living with you quite happily for some time since you and your husband split up, it would be extremely unlikely that the court would want to change this arrangement.

Other ways of getting custody

You can apply for custody of a child either in the magistrates' court, under the **Domestic Proceedings and Magistrates' Court Act 1978**, or to any court under the **Guardianship of Minors Act 1971**. The advantage of these proceedings are that they can be done at any time. You don't have to be getting a divorce.

DOMESTIC PROCEEDINGS AND MAGISTRATES' COURTS ACT 1978

If you make an application for maintenance (see Chapter 6), under this Act the magistrates' court will also look at custody and access arrangements. This will happen whether you wish it or not. The court cannot make an order for maintenance without looking at these arrangements first.

You can apply to the magistrates' court for maintenance for a child if your husband:

☐ doesn't reasonably maintain a child of the family;

☐ has behaved so that you cannot reasonably be expected to live with him;

☐ has deserted you;

☐ has failed to provide reasonable maintenance for you, depending upon your and his circumstances.

Maintenance can be paid in either regular instalments or in a single lump sum. Always consult a solicitor before issuing a summons, because the magistrates' court is limited in the amount of lump sum that they can award you, and you might be better off asking for maintenance in a different court.

GUARDIANSHIP OF MINORS ACT 1971

You can apply for custody, access or maintenance in any court under this Act unless you are still living together.

You may need to ask for custody very quickly, for example, if:

☐ you had to leave quickly and left the children behind;

☐ your husband has snatched the children and you want them back;

☐ you think your husband may take them out of the country.

You can use emergency procedures under the **Guardianship of Minors Act 1971** or you can start **wardship proceedings**.

Wardship proceedings are best, because the High Court has very wide powers indeed.

WARDSHIP PROCEEDINGS

You can apply to the High Court to have your child made a **ward of**

court. This means that your child is officially in the care of the High Court. S/he will still be allowed to stay with you, but no important decision can be made about him/her without the approval of the court. The child will become a ward of court as soon as the application is made. You can also apply for an injunction to protect the child immediately. The court has the power to warn the Home Office which can arrange for officials to keep a look out at ports and airports if you think the child may be taken out of the country. This does not always work in practice.

The hearing itself can be transferred to a local county court, where the court can:

☐ decide who shall have custody, care and control and access;

☐ award maintenance;

☐ place the child in the care of the social services department of the local authority (see Chapter 5).

The court can arrange for the child to have his/her own representative – a *guardian ad litem* (see page 30).

As you can see, there are several ways of making arrangements for your children. You should discuss with your solicitor which one would be best for you.

chapter five

Children in care

If your marriage has broken down, especially if there has been violence, one of the first things you will be concerned about is how to find a safe place for the children. You may have thought of asking the council's social services department to look after them – to take them into 'care' for a short time while you find more permanent accommodation. This may seem like a sensible idea, but you should be aware of the problems it may cause you.

Never put your children into voluntary care without getting advice from a solicitor.

The law on 'care'

The law relating to children is very complicated. There are several ways children can be placed in the care of the social services department:

☐ you can place your children in 'voluntary' care (see page 35);

☐ the council's social services committee can make a 'parental rights' resolution (see page 35);

☐ the council can apply to a juvenile court for a 'care order' (see page 36);

☐ the social services department can apply for a 'place of safety' order (see page 36);

☐ a court can decide to place a child in care during a custody hearing in matrimonial, guardianship or wardship proceedings (see Chapter 4). Children are placed in the care of the social services department of the council. Decisions are taken by a committee of elected members, but day-to-day work is carried out by individual social workers.

Voluntary care

The social services department have a duty to receive children into care if they haven't got a parent or guardian, or if you can't for some reason provide accommodation, maintenance or a proper upbringing. The social services department will only receive a child into care if it is the best course of action for *the child* to do so.

If the children are in care for less than six months, you should be able to take the children home at any time. If the children have been in care for more than six months then you will have to give the social services department concerned 28 days notice in writing that you want to take them home. While your children are in care the social services department may decide to try to keep your children in care, by making a parental rights resolution.

PROBLEMS OF VOLUNTARY CARE

Money
There may be problems with money. If you do not have your children with you, you will not be classed as a single-parent family, and you must sign on for work in order to claim Income Support (see page 55). If you are in work you will have to pay money to social services for the children's keep.

Housing
There may be problems with housing. If you apply to the council for housing because you are homeless, they may decide that you do not have a **'priority need'** and are not entitled to rehousing because the children are not with you (see page 20).

Rights of access
If you place your children in voluntary care you still retain all the parents' rights (see page 28). But you will *not* have any rights of access. You will have to come to an arrangement with the social worker about when you can see them (see page 38).

Think carefully before you put your children into care – there may be somewhere else safe for you all if you are homeless (see Chapter 2). It may count against you later if you want to apply for custody.

PARENTAL RIGHTS RESOLUTION
The social services committee can make a decision to take away your

parental rights and give them to the social services department. They can do this if your children are already in voluntary care and:

☐ you die, and there is no properly appointed guardian for your children;

☐ if you leave the children in voluntary care for three years;

☐ if they think that you have abandoned your children;

☐ if they think that you are an unfit parent, for example because of a physical or mental disability or because of your way of life;

☐ if parental rights have already been taken away from someone who lives, or is likely to live with you and your children.

The social services department has a duty to tell you when it makes a parental rights resolution. It is very important to keep them informed of your address if you move while your children are in voluntary care, because you only have fourteen days in which you can object to a parental rights resolution. If you do object in writing the resolution will end after fourteen days, unless the social services department decides to apply to the juvenile court for a care order. If you receive notice that the council has taken a parental rights resolution, go to an advice centre immediately. You can apply for Legal Advice and Assistance under the Green Form Scheme and for Legal Aid to be represented in court (see Chapter 1). You cannot remove your children from care while the case is waiting to come to court.

PLACE OF SAFETY ORDERS

A **place of safety** order is an emergency decision taken by a magistrate. It allows the social services to take your child away, without your consent, to a place of safety. This can be a police station, childrens' home, or foster home. The person applying for an order must have reason to believe that one of the grounds for making a care order exists (see page 37). A place of safety order lasts for 28 days and cannot be renewed. There is no appeal against it. Often the social services department will begin care proceedings if they have used one of these orders. If your child has been taken away from you by a place of safety order, then get legal advice immediately.

CARE ORDERS

Councils can only make a parental rights resolution for children who are already in their care. Sometimes they try to take children into care who are still living with their parents. In order to obtain a care order, the social services department would have to apply to the juvenile court. They have to show two things: first, that one of the grounds listed below exists, *and* second, that the child needs care and control which s/he won't receive at home. A care order can be made out on any of the following grounds:

☐ that your child's development or health is being neglected;

☐ that the health or development of another child in the same household was neglected;

☐ that someone who has been convicted of an offence against children is a member of your household, or is about to become a member of your household;

☐ that your child is in moral danger;

☐ that you can't control your child;

☐ that your child should be at school, and is not getting a proper education;

☐ that your child has committed an offence.

If the court believes that one of these grounds listed above is present, and that your child needs care and control which you are not able to give him/her, the court can decide to do any of the following:

☐ accept a sum of money from you as an undertaking that you will try to control your child. This is called a **recognisance**;

☐ order the social services department to supervise your child (in other words, visit and keep an eye on him/her);

☐ put your child into the care of the local social services department;

☐ appoint a guardian;

☐ if your child needs medical treatment, place him/her in a hospital.

In care proceedings, it is the child who is the subject of the proceedings, but you are usually allowed to represent him/her yourself. Sometimes the court will direct that your child should have his/her own representative, but you can still be present, and be represented. If the social services, or any other person begins care proceedings in relation to your child, get legal advice immediately. You can get Legal Aid to be represented in these proceedings. However, it is the child (not you) who is the subject of the proceedings, and so it is not possible for you to appeal against a decision of the court, unless the child's representative agrees to do so.

Guardianship, wardship and matrimonial proceedings

When you apply for custody, access or maintenance, you should be aware that the court does have the power to place your child in the care of the social services.

If you are applying to a court under the **Guardianship of Minors Act 1971** (see page 32); or to a magistrates' court under the **Domestic Proceedings and Magistrates' Courts Act 1978** (see page 32); or if you are having a hearing about arrangements for the children prior to your divorce (see page 30) the court can, in 'exceptional circumstances' make a care or supervision order on your child.

If the social services department haven't got the evidence to make a case to have your child taken into care in the magistrates' court, they may start **wardship proceedings** (see page 32). Anyone can start wardship proceedings, and once an application has been made to the High Court your child becomes a ward of court *straight away*. This means any important decisions which will affect the child's future have to be brought before the court.

You can get Legal Aid to be represented if your child is subject to wardship proceedings.

Access

One of the main problems where your child is taken into care will be getting to see your child. You do not have any automatic right of access to your child if s/he is in care. You have to make arrangements with your social worker. If you are not happy with the access arrangements that have been made for you, you have two ways of questioning them.

First, there is now a code of practice dealing with access arrangements which makes it clear that decisions about access need to be discussed with parents, and that a decision to stop you seeing your child altogether has to be made by the director of social services. You should take up your case with your local councillor first if you feel that the council's decision is unfair. You can find out who your local councillor is by telephoning the public information department of the council.

Second, if the council decides to end your access to your child, it must inform you in writing, and at the same time must explain to you that you have a right to apply to the juvenile court for access.

There is a list of useful addresses of places to go if you need to discuss a problem about care in Appendix 1.

chapter six

Maintenance

Maintenance is money which your husband pays to you on a regular basis (e.g. every week or every month). When you decide to separate, he may offer to pay you a regular sum to keep you and the children. If this is not enough, if it is not paid regularly or if he doesn't give you anything at all, you need to know how you can go about applying for maintenance.

Application to the magistrates' court

You or your solicitor can apply for maintenance to the magistrates' court if you can show any one of these:

☐ that your husband doesn't give you enough money to keep you or the children of the family;

☐ that your husband has behaved in such a way that you can't reasonably be expected to live with him;

☐ that your husband has deserted you;

☐ that you and your husband have separated by agreement for at least three months and your husband has been paying voluntary maintenance during that period.

The magistrate can order your husband to pay a regular sum. S/he can also order your husband to pay a lump sum of not more than £500 to clear some specific bill or debt, such as the gas bill, or a hire purchase debt. How much maintenance you will get depends upon a large number of things including what he can afford to pay. The most important thing which the magistrate will consider is the needs of any children of the marriage while they are under 17.

If your husband is willing to come to an arrangement to pay you and the children maintenance, you can also register a **maintenance agreement** in the magistrates' court.

The court will not necessarily approve the arrangement you have come to. If the magistrate thinks that the agreement does not give enough money to you and the children, and that your husband can afford more, then the magistrate can change the maintenance agreement.

Applications for maintenance in the magistrates' court can take time – about two months on average – and so the court can make an **interim order** – an immediate order until they have heard your case. An interim order can only last three months at the most although you can go back for one further order of three months.

The best thing about applications for maintenance in the magistrates' court is that your husband has to pay the court, not you. That way the court can keep a check on whether the order is being paid, and can write to your husband to chase him up if he doesn't pay. You will get your maintenance by cheque through the post, or you can collect it from the court if you prefer.

The divorce court can't do this for you, so if you have a maintenance order made for you and the children in the divorce court and your husband is not paying it, you should consider having it registered in the magistrates' court, because they can help make sure that it is paid.

Maintenance orders made in the magistrates' court can last up to, and after the divorce, or they can be for a fixed period of time (e.g. three years). The divorce court may decide on different arrangements.

Maintenance orders can be altered if either you or your husband apply to have them changed because of a change of circumstance such as your getting a job, or deciding to live with another man. Maintenance for you will end if you get married, unless an earlier time is stated in the order. Maintenance for your children will end once they reach 17, but the order can be extended if the children are in full-time education or training or in special circumstances such as the child having a disability.

Application to the divorce county court

It usually takes a long time for your divorce or judicial separation to get to the stage of a final decree, so the divorce county court has the power to make arrangements for maintenance until the decree absolute is granted. This can either by **maintenance pending suit** or **interim maintenance**. There are no guidelines on how much you should get if you apply for this.

The court can just make an order for as much or as little as it thinks reasonable. This will probably depend on what you need and on what your husband can afford.

Maintenance orders in the divorce court can be made at decree absolute, or at a decree of judicial separation (see pages 26 and 27), or at any time after that until you get remarried. If you have remarried you can still apply for maintenance for any children of the marriage.

Maintenance orders can be paid weekly, monthly or yearly.

How much will you get?

The court will have to look at a list of things when deciding how much you should have. First consideration will go to any children of the marriage while they are under 17. When deciding how much money is needed for the children, the registrar may have figures in front of him/her giving details of how much it costs to bring up a child. But the court will consider other things as well. These are listed below.

☐ The income and financial resources of both you and your husband. This can include any income you are likely to have, or could reasonably be expected to get in the future. This means that the court may look at your future earning capacity, and may consider it reasonable that you should return to work at some future date. It may be that you will have to produce evidence of the lack of opportunities for employment in your area. **Financial resources** can include a home if you and your husband own your own house. (If you and your husband are owner-occupiers, you should read Chapter 7 page 50 very carefully.)

☐ The financial needs of you and your husband. This means what you need to live on and what your husband's needs are, for example, if he has remarried and has a second family to support.

☐ The standard of living that you and your husband had before your marriage broke down.

☐ Your ages, and how long the marriage has lasted.

☐ Any physical or mental disabilities that you or your husband have.

☐ Any contribution that you or your husband have made to the welfare of the family, and any contributions that you are likely to make in the future. This means that if you have custody of the children, the court will take into account the fact that you will be looking after the children for some years to come.

☐ The conduct of you and your husband. Conduct will only be taken into account where it would be unfair to ignore it.

☐ The loss of any benefits that you might have had if the marriage had not broken down, for example, any pension scheme that your husband may belong to.

Obviously, it is very difficult for the court to take all these things into account and come to a simple answer. Some things will suggest that you should get more maintenance, others will suggest that you should get less.

There are some principles which may help to make this process of deciding how much maintenance you will get clearer.

First, the law says that the welfare of any minor children of the marriage will come first.

Second, a maintenance order should not make your husband's income go below what he would get on Income Support. This means that if your husband is now on Income Support you are unlikely to have maintenance given to you. You can still ask for a nominal order of, say, 5p per year which can be changed later if he does get a job.

Third, the law expresses the idea that if marriages are over, then there should be, if it is at all possible, a 'clean break' between the parties. So, if you are a young woman, and your marriage didn't last very long, and if there are no children, the court may decide to give you no maintenance at all, and end the financial relationship between you and your husband. However, if there are children, the court generally realises that it will be impossible to end the relationship between you and your husband. The court can also try to make a 'clean break' between you and your husband by ordering that he pay maintenance for a fixed time only (e.g. for three years).

Variation of maintenance orders

If your husband loses his job, or his financial circumstances alter, you or your husband can always go back to court to ask to have the order changed as long as your application was not dismissed in the first place. You can do this if there has been a change in any of the circumstances listed on page 41. That is why it is best always to ask for maintenance for yourself, even if it is only a little (e.g. 5p per year), so that if something *does* change, you can ask to have the order altered. In the same way, if your circumstances improve, your husband can apply to vary the maintenance order so that you get less. Some orders now may be for a fixed term only and may state that you can't go back to ask for more time.

Maintenance agreements

It is possible to come to a private agreement about maintenance in the divorce court (and also about other matters, such as housing, see page 40), and ask the judge to approve the agreement as a **consent order**. The judge will need to have a statement of your financial means, and those of your husband before s/he will approve the orders.

As most courts are very busy, they don't always get the chance to look as carefully at these arrangements as they should. Usually, if both sides have got solicitors, the judges will accept the agreement as it stands. But the judge does have very wide powers to alter agreements of this sort if s/he doesn't approve. For example, s/he is not likely to accept an agreement for you to go without maintenance if you are going to have to live on Income Support, unless you get some other substantial financial benefit such as a house. If you are considering an arrangement of this sort, read Chapter 8 carefully.

Most money matters – both maintenance and housing – are sorted out between solicitors, so it is very important that you should discuss it fully with your solicitor.

chapter seven

Long-term housing options

If you have found somewhere to stay temporarily while you sort yourself out, or if you do not feel the need to leave immediately but still feel that your relationship is breaking down, you will need to think about long-term solutions to your problems and your long-term rights to your home.

What you can do will depend on:

☐ whether you want to stay in the home;

☐ whether you are a council tenant, a housing association tenant, a private tenant or an owner-occupier.

Council tenants

RIGHT TO OCCUPY

Under the terms of the **Matrimonial Homes Act 1983**, both you and your husband have a right to live in the matrimonial home as long as you are married. Your husband cannot legally ask you to leave even if the tenancy is in his name (i.e. his name is on the rent book). Legally, he cannot be made to leave unless he is violent, or his behaviour is upsetting the children (see injunctions, page 7).

All council tenants have some measure of **security**. This means that the council cannot ask you to leave unless it applies to a county court for an order to evict you (called a **Possession Order**). The court will only order you to leave if the council proves that one of a number of grounds exist (for example, that you haven't paid the rent). If the council does send you a **notice** stating that they intend to go to court to try to evict you, go to an advice centre straight away.

RENT

If the tenancy is in your husband's name only, and he has left you, you can still remain. If your husband has not paid the rent, you are not legally responsible for the arrears. It may make things easier for you if you apply for Income Support and Housing Benefit to help you pay the rent (see page 61), because obviously the council will be happier with that arrangement. If the council does apply to the county court for a hearing because there are rent arrears, you can ask the court to **adjourn** (put off) the hearing until you have sorted out your matrimonial affairs.

If the tenancy is in your name only, or in both your names, then you are responsible for the rent. This includes any rent arrears, even if they are your husband's fault. If your husband has left you or is refusing to give you any money, you should apply straight away for Income Support or Housing Benefit (see pages 55 and 61). If you and your husband are joint tenants, some councils will agree to divide any rent arrears between you so that you will only have to pay half of them or even ignore them completely. But they don't have to do this. You are legally responsible for **all** of the rent.

TRANSFERRING THE TENANCY INTO YOUR SOLE NAME

If the tenancy is in your husband's name, or in the name of both you and your husband, you can get it transferred into your name only. There are two ways in which you can do this:

☐   If your husband agrees to transfer the tenancy to you he can **assign** (transfer) the tenancy into your name. This is done by a sealed document called a **deed**. Contact a solicitor and ask him/her to draw up a deed of assignment transferring the tenancy into your sole name. This can only be done as long as the council have never served you with a notice. Once you have the deed, take a copy to the council and ask them to change their records.

☐   If your husband does not agree to transfer the tenancy to you, you can ask the court to transfer it as part of your divorce or judicial separation proceedings. Your solicitor will apply to the court for a transfer of the tenancy under the **Matrimonial Causes Act 1973** or the **Matrimonial Homes Act 1983**. The court will look at what you and your husband need, and what other resources you have (e.g. income, savings etc). If you have children, the court will normally transfer the tenancy to the person who has been given custody of the children.

NB If the tenancy is only in your husband's name, it is very important to have the tenancy transferred to your name because otherwise your right to live there will end on divorce.

Housing Association tenants

If you live in a house or flat owned by a housing association and you moved in before 15 January 1989, your position will be the same as that of a council tenant described above.

If you moved in on or after 15 January 1989, however, your position will be slightly different because you will have an **assured tenancy** instead of a **secure tenancy**. This means that you will have slightly fewer rights. You will still have security – the housing association cannot ask you to leave without applying to a county court for an order to evict you, but it may be slightly easier for them to get one. It will also be more difficult for your husband to **assign** (voluntarily transfer) his tenancy to you. He will first have to get the housing association's permission. Your other rights and liabilities remain the same: the right to occupy, responsibility for rent and the right to ask the court to transfer the tenancy to your name (see council tenants above).

Private tenants

Whether or not you can stay in a private tenancy depends upon the agreement that you have with your landlord. The first thing that you need to do is to check whether you are what is called a **protected tenant** (if you moved in before 15 January 1989), or an **assured tenant** (if you moved in on or after 15 January 1989). If the following apply to you then you are probably a protected tenant or an assured tenant:

☐ your landlord does not live on the premises;

☐ you and your husband have a room of your own;

☐ your landlord does not provide services, such as clean sheets and towels, or room cleaning.

It is also important to check what your written tenancy agreement says, if you have one. If you moved in on or after 15 January 1989, you will need to check your agreement carefully to see whether you are an **assured shorthold tenant**. If you are, you will not have the same rights.

It is very important that you sort this out before you contact your landlord. The law in this area is very complicated. You can get advice on this from:

☐ a law centre, housing aid centre or Citizens Advice Bureau;

☐ the council's Tenancy Relations Officer (sometimes called the Harassment Officer);

☐ a solicitor.

If you are not a protected tenant or an assured tenant, then the landlord may not be willing to accept you as a tenant when your husband leaves. If he or she gives you notice to leave you should seek advice and you may be able to make an application to the council as a homeless person (see page 19).

If you are a protected tenant or an assured tenant, the following are your rights and responsibilities if your relationship breaks down:

RIGHT TO OCCUPY

Both you and your husband have a right to live in the matrimonial home as long as you are married, under the terms of the Matrimonial Homes Act 1983. Your husband cannot legally make you leave even if the tenancy is in his name (i.e. only his name is on the rent book). You cannot legally make him leave unless he is violent, or his behaviour is upsetting the children (see injunctions, page 7).

If you (or your husband) have a protected tenancy or an assured tenancy then you have some measure of security. This means that in order to evict you, your landlord must first apply to a county court for a **possession order**. It will be slightly easier for him or her to evict you if you have merely an assured tenancy rather than a protected tenancy. However, it will always be up to the court to decide. If your husband has left and the landlord applies to the county court for an order to evict you, you should get legal advice immediately. Remember, you have a right to remain there even if your husband leaves.

RENT

If the tenancy is in your husband's name and he has not paid the rent, you are not legally responsible for the arrears. If your landlord applies to the county court for an order to evict you, you can ask the court to adjourn (put off) the hearing until you have sorted out your matrimonial affairs. It may be a good idea for you to apply for Income Support and Housing Benefit to help you pay the rent as soon as possible (see Chapter 8).

If you are the tenant, or you and your husband are joint tenants, you are legally responsible for all the rent if he leaves. This includes any rent arrears even if they are your husband's fault. If your husband has left or is refusing to give you any money, you should apply immediately for Income Support, Housing Benefit or any other benefits to which you are entitled (see Chapter 8). If your landlord applies to the county court for an order to evict you (a possession order) you should get legal advice immediately.

TRANSFERRING THE TENANCY

If the tenancy is in your husband's name, or in the names of both you and your husband, you can get it transferred into your name only. Your solicitor can ask the court to transfer the tenancy into your name as part of your divorce or judicial separation proceedings, under the provisions of the Matrimonial Homes Act 1983 or the Matrimonial Causes Act 1973. The court will look at what you and your husband need, and what other resources you have (e.g. income, savings etc). If you have children, the court will usually transfer the tenancy to the person who has been given custody of the children.

NB It is very important to do this because, if the tenancy is in your husband's name, your rights to live there may end on divorce.

Moving

If you don't want to stay in the matrimonial home because your husband has been violent or has threatened violence to you or the children, then you should make an application to the council as a homeless person (see page 19). If there has been no violence, then these are the things you can do:

COUNCIL AND HOUSING ASSOCIATION TENANTS

Even if you don't want to live in your home any more, it is still worth having the tenancy transferred to your name when you apply for a divorce or judicial separation (see page 24). If you have nowhere else to go, the court will not be willing to allow your husband to have the tenancy if it will mean that you and your children will become homeless. But once you become the only tenant, there are ways that you can move home even though they may all take a long time. You can:

☐ apply to the council or housing association for a transfer;

☐ apply for a mutual exchange. This is where you find another tenant who is interested in swopping his or her property for yours. When you have found someone with whom you wish to exchange, you must both apply to your landlords for consent to the exchange. Your landlords must reply within 42 days of your application, saying if they agree or disagree to the exchange. If you are a housing association tenant and moved in on or after 15 January 1989, the rules on mutual exchanges may be different. You should check this with your Association. The grounds on which a landlord can refuse to allow a mutual exchange to go ahead are:

- that the tenant, or the person with whom s/he proposes to swop is to be evicted by a court order at some time in the future, or has been served with a notice telling them that the landlord intends to seek possession;

- that the accommodation is too large, or too small, for the needs of the proposed incoming tenant;

- that the landlord is a charity providing special accommodation, or for people in special circumstances, and the proposed incoming tenant is not one of these;

- that the accommodation is specially adapted (e.g. for the disabled) or is near special facilities (e.g. a day centre for the mentally ill) and the proposed incoming tenant doesn't need these things.

The landlord cannot refuse to agree to an exchange on any other ground.

☐ If you need to move a long distance to be near relatives, or to take up a job, you can apply under the **National Mobility Scheme** for a transfer.

PRIVATE TENANTS

If you are a protected or an assured tenant, you should still apply to have the tenancy transferred into your name as part of your proceedings for divorce or judicial separation. This may seem pointless if you do not wish to live there, but if you do not have anywhere else to go, the divorce court will not be willing to allow your husband to have the tenancy if you and your children are going to become homeless. It may also be very difficult for you to find somewhere else to live and you will need somewhere to stay whilst you look. To find alternative accommodation, you can:

☐ apply to the council to register on the waiting list;

☐ apply to a housing association or ask the council to nominate you to one;

☐ look for alternative private rented accommodation, although this will be very difficult as landlords are likely to charge high rents as well as wanting rent in advance, deposits and (after January 1989) **premiums** or **key money**, which is money paid for the 'granting' of the tenancy, as distinct from returnable deposits or rent in advance. It may be possible to apply to the Social Fund for some money for this, but it is very difficult to get it (see page 58).

Owner-occupiers

RIGHTS OF OCCUPATION

As long as your marriage continues, both you and your husband have a right to occupy the matrimonial home. He cannot legally make you leave, even if the house was bought in his name. You cannot legally make him leave unless he has been violent, or unless his behaviour has upset the children. Under these circumstances you might be able to get an injunction to get him to leave (see page 7).

If the house was bought in both your names, your husband cannot sell it without your knowledge and consent.

If the house was bought in your husband's name only, you must take action straight away, to protect your rights of occupation. You can stop your husband selling the house or raising another mortgage on it by **registering a charge**. This shows that you are claiming an interest in it.

HOW TO REGISTER A CHARGE

Your solicitor can register a charge for you. If you want to do it yourself, it is quite simple. Buy the **Land Registry Form No.96** at a law stationers (it costs only a few pence). Law stationers are listed in the **Yellow Pages**. Fill in the form and write across the top, 'This search is being made for the purposes of the Matrimonial Homes Act 1983'. Post it to your district land registry office (see Useful Addresses, Appendix 1). This will tell you whether your home is registered or unregistered land.

If it is **registered**, buy and complete **Land Registry Form 99** and send it with the necessary (small) fee to the chief land registrar at the same district land registry office as before.

If it is **unregistered**, you will have to register what is known as a **Class F Charge** at the Land Charges Registry. Again, all you have to do is complete a form. Buy **Land Charges Form K2**, complete it and post it to the Land Charges Department (see Useful Addresses, Appendix 1).

MORTGAGE PAYMENTS

You are entitled to make mortgage payments to the lender, even if the mortgage is in the name of your husband. If the lender refuses to accept money, draw their attention to **section 1(5)** of the **Matrimonial Homes Act 1983**. If they still refuse to accept payments, then keep the money in a separate account, so if your lender tries to take you to court you will be able to prove that you have been trying to pay. If you cannot afford the repayments, you should apply for Income Support and Housing Benefit for financial assistance (see page 56). You should write to your lender straight away to explain what has happened. You may be able to rearrange your mortgage so that you can afford it. There are several ways you can do this. Get advice from an advice centre or read SHAC's and CPAG's guide *Rights Guide for Homeowners* (see Useful Publications, Appendix 2).

If the lender does go to court to seek an order to evict you (called a **Possession Order**) you can go to court to ask the court to **adjourn** (put off) the hearing until you have sorted out your matrimonial affairs. If you do receive a summons for a court hearing, get legal advice immediately.

RIGHTS TO THE HOME
When you apply for a divorce or judicial separation, the court has wide powers to make orders about what entitlement you will have to any property or income that you and your husband hold. (For more information about income see Chapter 8).

When you and/or your husband own a house, this will count as 'property' which will be considered by the court. The court can order that the ownership of the house be transferred completely from one person to another, that the house be sold, or that it be sold at a later time.

It is best for you to know what the court can do, and how it decides what to do, so that you can choose the best solution for yourself. Remember, if you are worried that you won't be able to afford to keep the house on, you may be able to get financial assistance (see Chapter 8).

WHAT HAPPENS TO THE MATRIMONIAL PROPERTY?
The court looks at a list of things to decide how the matrimonial home should be divided. The court has a very difficult decision to make but the law says that *first* consideration must be given to any children of the marriage while they are under 18. After that, the court looks at:

☐ the income and resources of both you and your husband. This can include any income you are likely to have, or could reasonably be expected to get in the future. This means that the court may look at your future earning capacity, and may consider that it is reasonable to expect you to go back to work in the future. It may be that you will have to provide evidence of the lack of employment opportunities in the area;

☐ the needs of you and your husband. This means what you need to live on, and what your husband's needs are (e.g. if he has remarried and has a second family to support);

- [ ] the standard of living that you and your husband had before your marriage broke down;

- [ ] your ages, and how long the marriage lasted;

- [ ] any physical or mental disabilities affecting you or your husband;

- [ ] any contributions that you and your husband have made to the welfare of the family, and any contributions that you are likely to make in the future. This means, if you have custody of the children, the court will take into account the fact that you will be looking after the children for some years to come;

- [ ] the conduct of you and your husband. The behaviour of you and your husband will only be taken into account if the court thinks that it would be unfair to ignore it.

- [ ] the loss of any benefits that you might have had if the marriage had not broken down (e.g. any pensions scheme that your husband may belong to).

The court also have to consider whether there is any way that they can make a 'clean break' between you and your husband. This means ensuring that there would be no further financial ties between you and your husband.

HOW WILL A COURT ORDER BE ENFORCED?

Once it is decided *how much* of the value of the house you are entitled to, the court can decide *how* you will get it. For example, the house could be sold straight away, and you would get your share immediately. But unless you receive enough money to buy another house for you and your children it might be best to consider a different type of order. It is very important to remember that it is not usually possible to go back to court to change an arrangement about property. It is important to get it right first time. Here are some examples of arrangements that have been made in the past:

Sale 'deferred' for a time until some future event

This means that your share and your husband's share in the property are fixed, and that they will be paid to you and him when the house is sold. The house will not be sold until something happens – if you remarry, if you die, or if you decide yourself that you want to sell the house. Sometimes women have been ordered to pay rent to their ex-husbands once all the children are over 18.

Some courts and solicitors used to specify that the house would be sold when children reached the age of 18; but this is not a very good arrangement unless you can be sure that you will be able to afford to buy a new house for yourself afterwards. If you have this kind of order and you are worried that you will be in this position, get advice immediately.

Buy your husband out

When the court decides what your husband's share is and if you are in a position to raise enough money to pay him that share, the house could be transferred to you outright. But remember, never go to a finance company to raise a second mortgage. Try your present lender, or your bank or your local council. If they refuse, get advice from an advice centre. Finance companies usually charge very high interest, and you could find yourself in a nasty financial mess.

Have the house transferred to you and lower your claim for maintenance

This is called **trading off**. You tell the court that you will claim less maintenance if the house is transferred into your name. *Remember*:

☐ Maintenance is only useful if you receive it. If your husband is unlikely to pay regularly, or at all, you could be much better off with full ownership of the home. This sort of settlement fits in with the 'clean break' idea outlined above (see page 42). It is always however, worthwhile getting an order for even a token sum (e.g. 5p per year) as you can then apply to have the order varied if your husband's circumstances change for the better.

☐ If you are receiving Income Support, any maintenance you get will be taken off your Income Support entitlement. The value of the house, however, will not affect your Income Support; and Housing Benefit will help you pay the general rates.

☐ If you do decide to go for this option, it is helpful to get a letter from your solicitor stating that your husband is fulfilling his obligations to maintain you by giving you capital (in the form of the home) so that you won't become homeless. Unless the Department of Social Security (DSS) accept this they may take your husband to court for failing to maintain you.

These are the main ways of keeping your home. It is not easy to move unless both you and your husband can get enough money from the sale of the house to buy a house each. This does not happen very often.

The court has said in one case that it is not prepared to order a sale of a home so that one partner can make an application as homeless to the local council. It is also *not* a good idea to agree to a sale of your home if you have nowhere else to go. If you later have to apply to the council because you are homeless, they may decide that you are 'intentionally homeless' (see page 17). Also, if you sell your house at the time of the divorce, you will have to pay your Legal Aid costs straight away (see page 4). You may not get as much money as you first thought.

Remember: if you think that you cannot afford to keep the house on, try applying for Income Support, Family Credit and/or Housing Benefit (see Chapter 8).

chapter eight

Money

Because your income is likely to drop when a relationship ends, especially if you have children, it is important to check your financial situation very carefully and make sure you are being taxed correctly and claiming all the social security benefits you are entitled to.

The following chapter gives a basic outline of the main benefits you can claim and some ideas of how your claim will be assessed. It is important to get advice as the benefits system is complicated but could help you to maximise your income. Advice agencies who specialise in benefits are listed in Appendix 1.

If your stay in the U.K. is conditional on your not having 'recourse to public funds' or there is any question about your immigration status, before claiming anything seek advice from the Joint Council for the Welfare of Immigrants (see Useful Addresses, Appendix 1).

Income Support

This benefit replaced Supplementary Benefit on 1 April 1988.

Income Support is payable to those who work less than 24 hours in paid employment per week and

☐ have less than £6,000 capital;

☐ live in the U.K.

(If you have between £3,000 and £6,000 capital you can claim Income Support but it will be assumed that you earn £1 per week for every £250 *of that sum*.) This will then be deducted from your Income Support entitlement.

HOW INCOME SUPPORT IS CALCULATED

There are fixed amounts for each person in your household (see Appendix 3). You will get the allowance rate as shown for yourself and any children.

In addition, you may qualify for a **premium** which is an additional weekly payment for special circumstances. If you are a single parent, you will get the Family Premium and the Lone Parent Premium paid in addition to your weekly allowance (see Appendix 3). Other premiums depend on whether you or anyone in your family are disabled.

If you are living in board and lodging accommodation, your benefit will be calculated differently.

In addition, you may get an amount for housing costs if you claim for mortgage interest payments.

HELP WITH MORTGAGE PAYMENTS FROM INCOME SUPPORT

If you are paying a mortgage, Income Support will pay 50% of the interest payments for the first *sixteen weeks* of your claim, and the full amount thereafter as long as the loan was taken out to buy, improve or repair your home.

You can only get the full amount paid from the start of your claim if you are aged 60 or over.

Any interest on arrears which arises during the first sixteen weeks will be paid subsequently by the DSS.

If your husband has left and is not paying the mortgage – you can claim the interest on all loans as long as it is necessary for you to continue living there. If your husband was claiming Income Support for 16 weeks or more, and you make your own claim within 8 weeks of his leaving, the DSS should pay all of the interest payments on the mortgage(s).

If your husband was claiming Income Support for less than 16 weeks, and you make your own claim within 8 weeks of his leaving, you will get 50% of the interest on the mortgage(s) until the 16 week claim period has been completed.

The benefit paid will be for the interest part of your monthly repayments only and will not include the capital repayments. However, if you recently separated your lender should be willing to accept interest only payments for a period. The insurance premium part of an endowment mortgage will *not* be payable under Income Support. If you are separated from your partner, you can claim Income Support for interest payments on *any* loan payments which have to be met in order for you to continue living in the property if your partner cannot or will not make these payments (for example, if your partner has taken out a loan for his business you can claim for the interest repayments on that).

Note

You will have to meet at least 20% of the payment for your **general rates** from the amount calculated for your Income Support.

There is no longer a separate amount for **water rates** included in your Income Support and you will be expected to pay these from your allowance.

The total amount of your allowances and premiums and (if payable) housing costs is called your **applicable amount**.

From this, any income or other benefits will be deducted and the difference will be the amount of Income Support you are paid.

WHAT COUNTS AS INCOME?

☐ Child Benefit;

☐ One Parent Benefit;

☐ Pensions;

☐ Maintenance;

☐ Income from capital.

Any maintenance for you or your children is counted in full. If you are not getting your maintenance regularly, it is a good idea to get your maintenance order signed over to the DSS. If the maintenance order was made in the divorce court, you will have to get it registered in the magistrates' court. A lump sum payment of maintenance can lead to you losing benefit entirely for a period. However, if you use it to pay off debts, you should not lose benefit. Get advice from a local advice centre if you are worried about this.

Earnings

Your **net** earnings (i.e. take home pay) for any part-time work will be counted as income but **there is a £15 earnings disregard for single parents**. So if you take home £30 per week only £15 will be deducted from your Income Support.

Savings

If you have between £3,000 and £6,000 savings it will be assumed that you earn £1 for every £250 of this sum, which will be counted as income.

If you are living with a man as husband and wife, you will be treated as a single unit by the DSS and your *joint* income will be assessed.

WHAT DOES NOT COUNT AS INCOME?

☐ Housing Benefit;

☐ Mobility Allowance;

☐ Attendance Allowance;

☐ Social Fund Payments;

☐ Pensioners Christmas Bonus.

HOW TO CLAIM INCOME SUPPORT
You should fill in a claim form B1 from the Unemployment Benefit Office if you are not working.

If you are working you should get form SB1 from a post office or get in touch with the DSS and ask for an Income Support claim form.

Income Support is paid **two weeks in arrears** by girocheque posted to your address or by order book which can be cashed at the post office.

OTHER HELP FOR PEOPLE ON INCOME SUPPORT

☐ free prescriptions;

☐ free NHS dental treatment;

☐ travel to hospital for NHS treatment;

☐ help with the cost of glasses;

☐ help from the Social Fund.

The Social Fund

The Social Fund replaced the old single payments system in April 1988. It was set up to enable claimants to meet one-off expenses which would be difficult to pay out of their weekly benefit.

If you need to buy some essential furniture or need removal expenses, for example, the Social Fund **may** be able to help you.

The majority of payments are in the form of **loans**, and you will have to pay back the loan from your subsequent weekly benefit. So you need to bear in mind that your benefit will be reduced for some time afterwards if you get a loan.

There are three types of payment available from the Social Fund:

☐ Budgeting loans;

☐ Crisis loans;

☐ Community Care Grants.

Budgeting Loans are payable to people who have been claiming Income Support for 26 weeks to help them meet 'important intermittent expenses'. Savings over £500 will affect your claim. (Each DSS office has its own priorities for awarding the loans – you may need to get advice before applying.) There are some things, e.g. deposits for accommodation, for which you **cannot** claim a budgeting loan and different items have different priorities.

Crisis Loans are payable to 'meet expenses which arise in an emergency or as a consequence of a disaster'. **You do not have to be claiming Income Support to get a crisis loan**.

Community Care Grants are the only Social Fund payments which do not have to be repaid but there are quite specific qualifying grounds.

Community Care Grants are payable 'to assist an eligible person' where such assistance will:

i)   help that person re-establish him/herself in the community following a stay in institutional care; or

ii) help that person remain in the community rather than enter institutional care; or

iii) ease exceptional pressure on that person or their family; or

iv) help someone with travel expenses to visit an ill person or to attend a relative's funeral; or to ease a domestic crisis; or to visit a child who is with the other parent, pending a custody decision; or to move to suitable accommodation.

You may be able to get a grant if you have been living with your partner for at least three months and you have children and the relationship has ended or if you have no children but a 'longstanding' relationship which has recently ended. In cases of violence where your children may be at risk, you should be given priority.

Things for which you may get a Community Care Grant include removal expenses, clothing and footwear, or connection charges.

If you think you meet the criteria, you should apply for a grant rather than a loan. Get advice if you are unsure or need help with the application.

IMPORTANT NOTES ABOUT THE SOCIAL FUND

☐ **The Social Fund is discretionary**. This means you are not automatically entitled to a grant or loan. The Social Fund officer will consider all the relevant details and your individual circumstances.

☐ The Social Fund is cash-limited which means each DSS office has a budget which it cannot overspend and this will be a factor in deciding whether you get a loan/grant.

☐ There is no right of appeal from a Social Fund officer's decision, but you can ask for an independent review of the decision.

HOW TO APPLY
Fill in Form SF300 from the DSS office.

Family Credit

This benefit is for people who work **more than 24 hours per week**, have a capital of less than £6,000 and who are on a low income and caring for children.

It replaced Family Income Supplement (FIS) in April 1988.

'Children' includes young people up to 19 for whom the claimant receives Child Benefit. If there is some doubt as to which parent the child lives with, Family Credit will be paid to the parent who claims Child Benefit. You should not be treated as a couple if you and your partner have separated. Family Credit is paid for a 26week period from the date of claim. You will need to renew your claim four weeks before the end of each 26-week period.

HOW FAMILY CREDIT IS WORKED OUT

1) *Capital*
If you have capital of between £3,000 and £6,000, it will be assumed that you have an income of £1 per week for every £250 of this sum. If you have more than £6,000 capital you cannot claim Family Credit.

2) *Income*
Your total income will be calculated including net earnings, some benefits, maintenance payments and income from capital. Child Benefit, One Parent Benefit, Mobility Allowance, Attendance Allowance and Housing Benefit are **ignored** as income for Family Credit purposes.

3) There is a fixed Family Credit **threshold** of £54.80 (from 10 April 1989).

4) There are set amounts of credits for you and the children in your household.

Claimant	£33.60 (single claimant or couple)
Child under 11	£ 7.30
11–15	£12.90
16–17	£16.35
18	£23.30

If you add together the appropriate credits for your family this will give you your **maximum Family Credit**.

5) Your income will be compared with the threshold figure of £54.80.

If your income is less than £54.80
You will receive your maximum Family Credit.

If your income is more than £54.80
You will receive maximum credit less 70% of the difference between your income and £54.80.

HOW TO CLAIM FAMILY CREDIT

Fill in Form FC1 from the DSS office or Post Office.

Family Credit can be paid direct to your bank account or by order book.

OTHER HELP FOR PEOPLE RECEIVING FAMILY CREDIT

☐ Free NHS prescriptions;

☐ Free NHS dental treatment;

☐ Travel to hospital for NHS treatment.

Family Credit claimants will **not** get free school meals.

Housing Benefit

This is a government scheme to help people, who are either unemployed or on a low income, pay their rent and rates. It is run by local councils.

Housing Benefit can be paid to council tenants and private tenants for rent and rates or owner-occupiers for help with rates.

People with capital of more than £8,000 cannot claim Housing Benefit.

IF YOU ARE CLAIMING INCOME SUPPORT

A form to claim Housing Benefit should be included in your Income Support claim form which will be forwarded by the DSS to your local council.

If you are receiving Income Support, you should get maximum Housing Benefit

☐ 100% of your rent;

☐ 80% of your rates;

☐ less deductions for any adults living with you.

You are expected to pay the remaining 20% of your rates from your Income Support.

IF YOU ARE NOT ON INCOME SUPPORT

You will have to complete a form from your local council offices. Whether you are entitled to Housing Benefit or how much you will get will depend on:

☐ The amount of rent and rates you pay.

☐ The number of people in your household. Generally, if you have dependent children, your benefit will be increased. But if there are other adults, including boarders or sub-tenants, in your household, your benefit will be reduced.

☐ The amount the law says people need to live on (see Appendix 3).

☐ Your income from other benefits, or maintenance payments. (NB: Mobility Allowance and Attendance Allowance will not count as income.)

☐ Your income from earnings. (NB: There is a £15 disregard for single parents.)

☐ Income from capital. If you have less than £3,000, this won't affect your Housing Benefit. If you have between £3,000 and £8,000 it will be assumed that you earn £1 per week in interest for every £250 of that sum.

HOW HOUSING BENEFIT IS PAID

Council tenants

Your Housing Benefit will automatically reduce the amount of rent you need to pay the council. This way, you will not actually receive any money yourself.

Private/housing association tenants or owner-occupiers

Your Housing Benefit can be paid either by regular giro cheque, or directly into a bank account. The money is payable to you, rather than the landlord.

BENEFIT ON TWO HOMES

There are rare circumstances in which the council will pay rent on two homes; one of these is if you have left your previous home and remain absent from it through fear of domestic violence.

This is an important provision because it prevents you from getting into rent or mortgage arrears if you have to leave home because of violence.

Child Benefit

Child Benefit is an allowance paid to people bringing up children aged 16 or under, or aged up to 18 and in full-time education.

It is a non-means tested benefit which means you can claim it whether you are working or unemployed, and regardless of how much you earn.

The present rate of Child Benefit is **£7.25 per week** for each child.

You can claim it by filling in a form available either at the Post Office or from the DSS.

It is normally paid four weeks in arrears.

One Parent Benefit

Single parents are also entitled to claim an additional sum for bringing children up on their own. The current rate of One Parent Benefit is **£5.20 per week** (from 10 April 1989) which is a flat rate, however many children you have.

Note

You may choose not to claim One Parent Benefit if this will take your income above the level where you can receive Income Support, as Income Support entitles you to free school meals and prescriptions.

Tax

The tax year runs from 6 April to 5 April of the following year. Each tax year, you are allowed to earn a certain amount before you are liable to pay tax – this amount is your **tax allowance**.

A single parent can claim a **single persons tax allowance** and an **additional persons allowance** which is payable to people bringing up a child under 16 alone. If you and your ex-partner share the care of your child, the allowance can be split between you.

If you are living with your partner and have more than one child, you can both claim an additional persons allowance up to April 1989. After this date only one partner can claim.

MORTGAGE INTEREST TAX RELIEF

Tax relief on your mortgage payments is usually deducted at source under the MIRAS scheme. This means you automatically pay reduced payments to your lender. MIRAS is available up to £30,000.

MAINTENANCE FOR MARRIED WOMEN

A detailed explanation on how to claim maintenance from your husband is contained in Chapter 6.

The arrangements for taxing maintenance payments has become more complicated since the budget of 1988.

The arrangements for taxing maintenance payments will now depend on:

1) whether the maintenance order was taken out before or after 15 March 1988;

2) whether the payment is voluntary or enforceable (i.e. made in court);

3) whether you are married or not.

The information given here relates to *married partners.*

If your order was made before 15 March 1988

Voluntary payments agreed between you and your ex-husband outside court do not qualify for tax relief and you are not liable for tax on any maintenance you receive. (This remains the same under the new rules.)

Enforceable orders

A maintenance order taken out under the old system means that the maintenance payment is counted as your taxable income, so any income above your tax allowance, including maintenance, will be taxed accordingly. Under this system, your ex-husband can claim tax relief on the maintenance he pays to you. For a small maintenance payment (£25 per week or less paid to you), your ex-husband will claim tax relief by an adjustment to his tax code. For large payments (£25 per week or more paid to you) tax relief is obtained by your ex-husband deducting the tax directly from the payments he makes to you.

If however the order is made directly to your child instead of to you, it will not count as your taxable income and it is considered as your child's income. It is therefore a good idea to have your maintenance paid this way under the old system.

If your order was made after 15 March 1988

Any order made after this date will be subject to the new rules as follows:

☐ Your ex-husband will be able to claim tax relief up to a maximum of £1,490 a year on maintenance he pays to you for yourself or your child.

He will not be able to claim any tax relief on maintenance payments paid direct to your child.

☐ You will not have to pay tax on any maintenance you receive (up to £1,490).

EXISTING ORDERS

☐ All orders replaced or varied after March 1988 are subject to the new rules.

☐ For existing orders in the tax year 1988/89 – your ex-husband will be taxed as before including relief on payments made directly to a child. After April 1989, he will be taxed as the previous year up to the new tax limit (£1,490) even if he increased the payments.

☐ You will still be liable to tax on payments to yourself as in previous years but from April 1988 the first £1,490 will be tax-free. From April 1989, you are only liable for tax on payments up to the level which was taxable in 1988/89, with the £1,490 exemption.

appendix one

Useful addresses

The best place to get detailed advice on a complex problem, if not from your solicitor, is from a local advice agency. The agencies listed below are nation- or London-wide but should be able to give help or refer you. Your local Citizens Advice Bureau (CAB) or housing aid centre should be listed in the telephone directory.

BENEFITS

Child Poverty Action Group
(CPAG)
1–5 Bath Street
London EC1V 9QA
☎ (01) 253 6569

HOUSING

SHAC
(The London Housing Aid Centre)
189a Old Brompton Road
London SW5 0AR
☎ (01) 373 7276

IMMIGRATION & related issues

Joint Council for the Welfare
of Immigrants
115 Old Street
London EC1V 9JR
☎ (01) 251 8706

GENERAL

National Association of
Citizens Advice Bureaux
Myddleton House
115–123 Pentonville Road
London N1 9LZ
☎ (01) 833 2181

Gingerbread
(support group for single parents)
35 Wellington Street
London WC2
☎ (01) 240 0953

Lesbian Line
BM Box 1514
London WC1N 3XX
☎ (01) 837 8602

Maternity Alliance
15 Britannia Street
London WC1X 9JP
☎ (01) 837 1265

Family Rights Group
6–9 Manor Gardens
Holloway Road
London N7 6LA
☎ (01) 272 7308

Childrens Legal Centre
20 Compton Terrace
London N1 2UN
☎ (01) 359 6251

One Parent Families
225 Kentish Town Road
London NW5
☎ (01) 267 1361

Womens Aid Federation (England)
PO Box 391
Bristol BS99 7WS
☎ (0272) 420611
    (Admin and Information)
    (0272) 428368
    (National Helpline)

Womens Aid Federation (Wales)
34–48 Crwys Road
Cardiff
South Glamorgan CF2 4NN
☎ (0222) 390874/390875
    (0222) 390878 (Housing Line)

12 Cumbrian Place
Aberystwyth, Dyfed
☎ (0970) 612748/611307

Womens Advice Centre
c/o Manor Gardens Centre
6–9 Manor Gardens
London N7 6LA
☎ (01) 281 2205

Rights of Women
52–54 Featherstone Street
London EC1Y 8RT
☎ (01) 251 6577

Latin American Womens Rights
    Service
Priory House
Kingsgate Place
London NW6 4TA
☎ (01) 372 6408

Chiswick Family Rescue
*(emergency accommodation and
advice)*
PO Box 855
London W4 4JF

LAW (Legal Action for Women)
(free legal advice for women)
Kings Cross Womens Centre
71 Tonbridge Street
London WC1H 9DZ
☎ (01) 837 7509

Land Registry
Lincoln's Inn Fields
London WC2
☎ (01) 405 3488

General Register Office
(Births, deaths & marriages)
St Catherines House
10 Kingsway
London WC2
☎ (01) 242 0262

Useful publications

National Welfare Benefits Handbook, Child Poverty Action Group, 1–5 Bath Street, London EC1V 9PY   Price £5.50

Rights Guide to Non-Means Tested Social Security Benefits, Child Poverty Action Group, 1–5 Bath Street, London EC1V 9PY   Price £4.50

Housing Rights Guide, SHAC, 189a Old Brompton Road, London SW5 0AR   Price £5.95

Rights Guide for Homeowners, SHAC, 189a Old Brompton Road, London SW5 0AR   Price £4.50

Owning Your Flat: A Guide to Problems with your Lease and Landlord, SHAC, 189a Old Brompton Road, London SW5 0AR   Price £2.50

Guide to Housing Benefit and Community Charge Benefit, SHAC, 189a Old Brompton Road, London SW5 0AR   Price £6.50

Divorce – Legal Procedures and Financial Facts, Consumers Association, 14 Buckingham Street, London WC2

Publications available from National Council of One Parent Families, 255 Kentish Town Road, London NW5 2LX. All NCOPF publications are free to one-parent families.

Legal Rights of Single Mothers	£1.40
Single and Pregnant	£1.30
Social Security Benefits Rates	40p
Tax in 1988/89 (annually updated)	40p
Legal Aid	40p

Legal Advice and Assistance   40p
Income Support and the Social Fund   40p
Housing Benefit   40p
Help for the Homeless   40p
Child Benefit and One Parent Benefit   30p

Benefit Rates (from April 1989)

Child Benefit

For each child £7.25

One Parent Benefit

One Parent Benefit £5.20

Family Credit

If your net income exceeds £54.80 per week you will receive maximum credit less 70% of the difference between net income and £54.80.

You will be able to get the maximum amount of Family Credit if your net income is **£54.80** or less per week. The maximum rate is made up of the following:

Adult credit (amount for 1 to 2 parents) £33.60

plus for each child aged:

under 11 .... £ 7.30

11–15 .... £12.90

16–17 .... £16.35

18 .... £23.30

Housing Benefit

The maximum Housing Benefit you can get is 100% of your eligible rent and 80% of your eligible rates. The rates used to calculate your Housing

Benefit payments are generally the same as the allowances and premiums that make up Income Support (see page 72).

DEDUCTIONS FOR NON-DEPENDANTS
Taken from rent rebates and allowances

Aged 18 or over and in remunerative work .... £ 9.15

Boarders .... £ 9.15

Others (excluding 18–25 year olds in receipt of IS) .... £ 3.85

Low earnings threshold £52.10

Taken from rates rebates aged 18 or over .... £ 3.35

PREMIUM
Lone parent (Housing Benefit) .... £ 8.60

AMENITY DEDUCTIONS

Heating .... £ 7.00

Hot water .... £ 0.85

Lighting .... £ 0.55

Cooking .... £ 0.85

All Fuel .... £ 9.25

Income Support

Personal allowances, premiums and payments to cover certain housing costs together make up your benefit payment.

PERSONAL ALLOWANCES
Single

aged 16–17 .... £20.80

aged 18–24 .... £27.40

aged 25 or over £34.90

Couple

both aged under 18 .... £41.60

one or both aged 18 or over £54.80

Lone parent

aged 16–17 .... £20.80

aged 18 or over £34.90

Dependent children & young people

aged under 11 .... £11.75

aged 11–15 .... £17.35

aged 16–17 .... £20.80

aged 18 .... £27.40

PREMIUMS

Family .... £ 6.50

Lone Parent .... £ 3.90

Pensioner

single £11.20

couple £17.05

Higher pensioner

single £13.70

couple £19.50

Disability

single £13.70

couple £19.50

Severe disability

single £26.20

couple (if one qualifies) £26.20

couple (if both qualify) £52.40

disabled child .... £ 6.50

HOUSING COSTS DEDUCTIONS FOR NON-DEPENDANTS

18 or over and in remunerative work .... £ 9.15

Others (excluding 18–25 year olds in receipt of IS) .... £ 3.85

Low earnings threshold £52.10

HOSTELS AND BOARD & LODGING ACCOMMODATION

The maximum amount for board & lodging accommodation and meals is between **£45** and **£70**. The maximum amount for hostel accommodation and meals is **£70**.

ALLOWANCES FOR PERSONAL EXPENSES FOR CLAIMANTS IN HOSTELS

Lower personal expenses

single £11.95

couple £23.90

Higher personal expenses

single £13.25

couple £26.50

Expenses for dependent children

under 11 .... £ 4.10

11–15 .... £ 6.05

16–17 .... £ 7.00

18 .... £11.95

Glossary

access
the right of a parent who is not living with their children to visit their children

affidavit
a true statement sworn on oath.

assignment
where your husband voluntarily gives you his tenancy when he leaves. He will usually have to get his landlord's permission to do this.

assured tenant
if you rent accommodation from a private landlord or a housing association and you moved in on or after 15 January 1989 you will probably have an assured tenancy provided your landlord does not live on the premises and you do not receive any services (laundry, cleaning).

Attendance Allowance
money you can claim if you are severely disabled, mentally or physically, so that you require help from another person by day and by night to attend to your needs.

board and lodging accommodation
the DSS define this as a guesthouse, hotel, lodging house or accommodation which includes cooked meals as part of the rent as long as it is on a commercial basis. If you live in this type of accommodation you will probably be treated as a *boarder* and your Income Support is calculated differently from *householders*.

capital
your savings. Other things which the DSS may count as capital are property, shares, business assets.

care and control	the person who is responsible for the physical welfare of the child has care and control.
caution	a record listed at the Land Registry showing you have an interest in the property even if it is owned by your husband and he has left. A 'caution' has the same effect as a 'charge' (see below).
chambers	a room in the court where your case can be heard without members of the public being present.
charge	a record listed at the Land Charges Registry showing you have an interest in the property even if it is owned by your husband and he has left. Prospective purchasers will be informed of this to stop the property being bought over your head. The 'charge' will also prevent your husband raising further loans using the property as security.
conciliation	where the court holds a meeting with you and your husband to try to sort out what is going to happen to your children when you divorce.
consent order	if you and your husband come to an agreement about how much maintenance he will pay you, you can ask the judge in the divorce court to approve it.
corespondent	a term referring to the person against whom divorce proceedings are being taken.
custodian	someone who has obtained a Custodianship Order. This will give them parental rights in respect of a child. Custodianship is usually granted to a relative of the child, or foster parents.
custody	the right to have the child in your care and to make decisions about the child. Custody can be given to either a parent, or a relative.
decree absolute	the final order for divorce bringing your marriage to an end.
decree nisi	an order from the court allowing you to apply for a decree absolute to bring your marriage to an end.
deed	a signed document which is legally binding.

defended divorce	where your husband states that he does not consider the relationship to be at an end and does not want a divorce, and/or challenges the grounds on which you have applied for a divorce.
divorce court	the County Court or High Court in which the divorce hearing is heard.
exclusion order	see ouster order.
ex parte hearing	a hearing in court where only one party is present. If you have suffered domestic violence, you can have a hearing for an injunction without your husband or partner being present.
express trust	a written agreement defining what shares in the property each party is entitled to. The agreement may also set out how the property should be used and when it should be sold.
Family Credit	money paid to you to supplement your income if you have children and are in low paid employment and work for less than 24 hours per week.
Green Form	free initial advice from a solicitor (usually about 2–3 hours work). You will have to fill out a Green Form.
gross income	your income before tax is deducted.
guardian ad litem	someone appointed as the guardian of your child for the purposes of a court case (often a social worker).
Housing Benefit	help towards your housing costs for rent and/or rates if you are unemployed or on a low income.
household	you and the people you are claiming for are treated by the DSS as a single unit called a *household*. If you are living separately from your husband or partner, you should not be treated as part of the same household.
implied trust	someone who is not the owner of the property may have an interest in it if they can show an 'implied trust' has been created because they have contributed directly to mortgage payments, repairs or improvements or by providing a deposit.

income	the money you have coming in to your household from earnings, benefits, maintenance. Income is treated differently by the DSS for different benefits.
Income Support	money from the government paid to you if you do not work and are not supported by your husband.
institutional care	eg a residential care home for the elderly, disabled or mentally ill.
interest	money earned on capital in banks, building societies, etc.
injunctions	an emergency order from the court telling someone to do or not to do something. If your husband or partner has been violent to you, you can get an injunction telling him to leave your home, or not to come near you or your children.
Legal Aid	financial assistance with legal costs for people on low incomes.
licensee	someone living in a property with the permission of the tenant or landlord who may pay rent or may not. The law does not give a licensee any long term rights in the property; they must leave once they have been given reasonable notice (usually a few weeks).
maintenance	money paid to you by your ex-husband/partner for yourself and/or your child.
MIRAS	Mortgage Interest Relief at Source is the tax relief you receive on the interest you pay on the first £30,000 of your mortgage.
National Mobility Scheme	a scheme whereby you can apply for council housing in a different area or different part of the country, especially if you need to move for reasons of work or to look after an elderly or disabled relative.
net income	your income after tax and National Insurance contributions have been deducted.
ouster order	an order from the court telling your husband or partner to leave your home because he has been violent towards you or the children. He will usually be told to leave for 3 months.

paternity	establishing paternity means proving someone is the true father of a child. The court has the power to order a blood test to prove paternity in some cases.
petition	an application for divorce.
place of safety order	an emergency decision made by the court allowing the social services department to take your child away without your consent.
possession order	A court order saying you must leave your accommodation by a certain date, and giving possession of your accommodation back to your landlord (or lender if the property is mortgaged). Your landlord or lender cannot make you leave your accommodation until the court has granted this order.
premium	a non-returnable sum of money which a landlord may ask you for when you first move in to rented accommodation; OR – an additional amount paid on top of your Income Support or Housing Benefit rate e.g. for families, lone parents, pensioners or people with disabilities.
protected tenant	if you moved in to your accommodation before 15 January 1989 and you rent it from a private landlord you will probably be a protected tenant provided your landlord does not live on the premises and you do not receive any services (laundry, cleaning, meals).
recognisance	where you pay the court a sum of money as an undertaking that you accept responsibility for your child and will try to control him or her.
recourse to public funds	it is a condition of some people's stay in Britain that they are able to support themselves without financial assistance from central or local government. Claiming Income Support, Family Credit or Housing Benefit counts as having recourse to public funds, as does making an application to a local council as a homeless person (but making a waiting list application does not count).

registrar an officer of the court who will conduct an informal hearing of your case.

sub-tenant someone who lives with a tenant and pays them rent.

supervision order an order made by the court if it considers there are problems with your child. The order instructs social services to visit and keep an eye on your child.

undefended divorce where your husband does not object to you divorcing him.

index